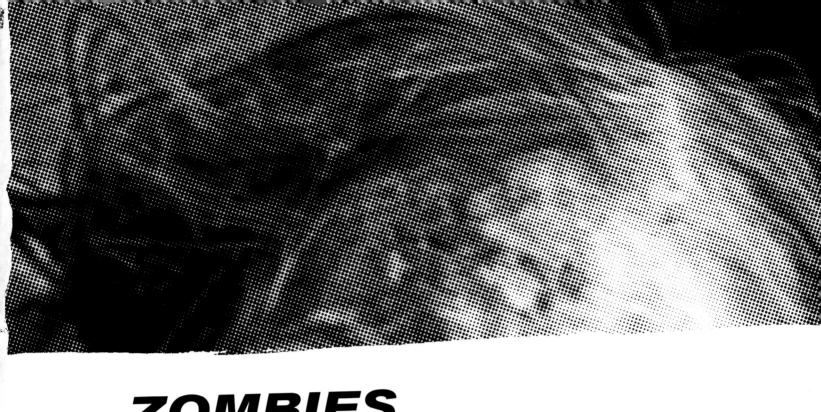

ZOMBIES

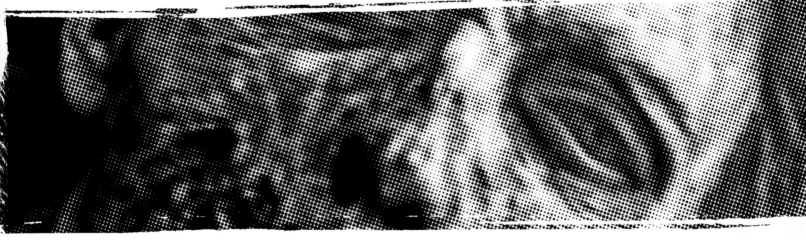

ON FILM

The Definitive Story of Undead Cinema

Universe

This edition published in the United States of America in 2014
by Universe Publishing,
A Division of Rizzoli International Publications, Inc.
300 Park Avenue South
New York, NY 10010
rizzoliusa.com

Edited by Robb Pearlman

Foreword Illustrations by Ashley Perryman Quach,
sassquach.com

All images appear courtesy of Photofest.

Printed in China

ISBN: 978-0-7893-2739-0
Library of Congress Control Number: 2014936609

ZOMBIES

ON FILM
The Definitive Story of Undead Cinema

By Ozzy Inguanzo
Foreword by Max Landis
Design by Chris McDonnell

Universe

ACKNOWLEDGMENTS

To Robb Pearlman at Rizzoli, for his undying support and commitment to this book.

Thanks to Chris McDonnell for delivering a classy yet eerie design.

My deepest gratitude to Max Landis, for sacrificing mankind in order to contribute an incomparable foreword. And to Ashley Perryman Quach for her playful depictions of humanity's last days.

A special thank-you to the staff of the Margaret Herrick Library at the Academy of Motion Picture Arts and Sciences.

Many thanks to François Audouy, Jessica Fuller, Bob Murawski, Rosa Palomo, Paul Quach, Elizabeth Smith, Carlene Tiedemann, Buddy Weiss, and to my parents Osvaldo and Juanita Inguanzo for their love and support.

DEDICATION

This book is dedicated to the creative, resourceful, and entrepreneurial spirit of the many independent filmmakers throughout the years whose combined talents and hard work have built an immortal motion picture legacy that will continue to entertain and terrify audiences for generations to come.

FOREWORD

Hello, my name is Max Landis, and I suppose there's really only one way to start this, and that's by saying I'm very sorry that I ended the world.

It stemmed from a desire to look clever, really. My entire adult life I've been congratulated for my intelligence and insight, but I've never felt particularly intelligent or insightful, especially in the shark tank of cynical, philosophically driven minds I've found myself surrounded by on blogs and in books, the literati sub-elite who populate pop culture and entertainment websites.

What I'm saying is that as a writer, I'm a bit of an optical illusion; I have the air and manner of a person with a great deal to say, but the hot air inside of the balloon of opinion and over-articulated thoughts about super heroes, science fiction, and fantasy is just that: hot air. What I'm saying is I wouldn't be asked to write an article in *Vanity Fair*, *New Yorker*, or *Playboy*, because at the end of the day my simple-palate communicative prose flatly just isn't that good. What I'm saying is that my talent as a screenwriter, already a medium where it's very easy to be bad and measurements of what's good feel very, very ambiguous, don't translate to this.

What are you reading this on, by the way? It can't be digital. Is it on the cardboard box I'm writing it on now? Or has the confession of the world's greatest murderer been transcribed somewhere?

What I'm saying is that if you asked me to write a foreword for a book about the zombie phenomenon in our culture, I'd probably just say no, because I'd be so intimidated by the absolute blundering wealth of cultural intellect already poured

onto that topic in the last ten years alone. In fact, along with Pirates and Ninjas, Zombies had, in my original timeline (before the incident), reached a really played-out "Go the hell away" status in pop culture.

The resurgence of zombie films in the early 2000s coincided painfully with the rise of social media, and the "ME ME MY OPINION LOOK HERE I'M INSIGHTFUL" phenomenon. Everyone became aware of the idea that the zombies themselves were secondary to the natural-disaster-type situation their presence created. Everyone slowly got the theme of zombies being more like a flood or a fire, and the notion that THE REALLY DANGEROUS THING IN ZOMBIE MOVIES IS THE OTHER SURVIVORS.

The culture caught on in a big way that zombies are an elemental representation of death; a primal nightmare that draws on our basic human-as-an-animal fears (death, disease, being eaten) and personifies them in a deeply nightmarish way. We had movies with zombie protagonists, we had movies with guys raping zombies, we had the entire Marvel Universe taken over by zombies. . .

See what I'm saying here? I was desperate. It wasn't often that I was approached by people to write forewords, or really, anything that forced me to step outside of my comfortable screenplay format. The Landis thing was my only connection; *Thriller* was my only option, and the bender seemed like the only way to get new information about that very overdocumented piece of my father's life. Don't you see? You must understand, I just wanted to seem smart. I just wanted to seem important.

Everything interesting to be said about zombies, from Mary Shelley to George Romero to Edgar Wright, has been said a million times, and loudly. "Jesus was a zombie!" people yelled, sure that this was the first time this idea had been mulled, and they sold T-shirts, so many T-shirts. "Nazi zombies!" yelled another crop.

"There've never been zombies that run before!" People raved about *28 Days Later*, somehow oblivious to literally dozens of movies where zombies ran or even displayed supernatural speed throughout the 20th century.

"They're not zombies, they're infected!" decried another slew of very passionate people, somehow ignoring the fact that a trope is a trope and *28 Days Later* is most definitely a freaking zombie movie, and if it's mostly brain-dead and comes at you in big groups trying to infect you with something that turns you into one of it, it's a ZOMBIE.

Zombies were so damn played out that by 2014, *The Walking Dead*, the most successful television show in the world, refused to use the word "Zombie," choosing instead to call them "walkers" or "biters." This is how sick with insight the world had become.

Figuring out time travel wasn't hard; there'd been a really amazing amount of research already done in Sweden, and my life's earnings as a screenwriter were a small price to pay a lone, radical inventor living on the fringes of society to fund a test. I figured, why did it matter, right? Surely if he created a device that worked I'd be able to use it to get as much money as I could ever want. Surely even the concepts of money and possession would be rendered meaningless or at least changed utterly by the reality of a time machine.

I thought I had it all figured out. I would look very smart, as well as impress everyone with my close relationship with my father, himself a celebrity in his time and a respected legend in mine, a man whose dalliances with zombies, horror, and comedy had led with no small amount of linear directness to the iconic zombie film *Shaun of the Dead*. An exclusive interview with John Landis and Michael Jackson from the set of the music video *Thriller*? Plus the added bonus of having figured out how to unstick from time and wander freely throughout the cosmos, a god on earth and maybe even off it, sovereign over all the societies of man from primeval times to the direst black of human infinity?

This was going to be a great foreword. Everyone was going to think I was really, really cool.

You can see here, already, the problem. I wasn't looking close enough. I was betraying the shallow intellectual depth that had led me into trouble my entire life. I wasn't paying attention to the details, and in doing so, was making the same dumb mistake people make as they caustically discuss the finer philosophical points of horror.

Like why did zombie films come back so big after 9/11? There are lots of theories. I have my own, and it's not about the primal fears of humanity, or horror at all really. It's about individuality. More than ever, in Western culture, we are urged to express ourselves, to shout our opinions; ever since MySpace made Warhol's fifteen-minutes-of-fame prediction into a living, breathing phenomenon, we've been hurtling towards a singularity, separating ourselves from each other while simultaneously putting more and more of our thoughts out into the demoralizingly public void of the Internet, the new human overmind.

Zombies represent the ultimate failure of individuality, worse even than the spectacular "Red Menace" of Communism, or even the frightening fanaticism of religious zealots. There's something that endlessly compels us about changing, metamorphosizing. For something that's supposed to be scary, there sure do seem to be a lot of people who think it would be pretty fun to be a werewolf, and pretty damn sexy to be a vampire. The known-unknown in the age of the Me Me Me culture has become desirable; Lord knows, being a werewolf would get you a hell of a lot of Twitter followers.

More than ever, everyone wants to be special.

But no one wants to be a zombie.

Barring some notable exceptions (*Return of the Living Dead 3* a standout), being infected by a zombie is almost always presented as the death of a person's personality, the rape-murder of their very soul. You aren't sleeping. You aren't coming back. You're just another face in a crowd. Another hungry mouth. No likes. No retweets. No blogs, no selfies. No more you. You're worse than dead: you're anonymous.

No one wants to be a zombie.

But everyone wants to be a survivor.

Take the Zombie Survival Quiz! Who Is Your Zombie Survival Team? Which of your friends do you think are special and interesting enough not to be eaten alive? Wow, cool zombie survival weapon! You're so brave! **You're** so tough! **<u>You're</u>** so smart!

You're a survivor. You have no workable skills. You spend all day on your phone. You don't do jack that would really help anyone. But you're a survivor. Haven't you seen zombie movies? Even without any sex, there is nothing sexier than survival. Nothing more primal. Work as a unit, not with the species, just you and your friends, and anyone who doesn't cooperate is the villain.

Zombies aren't a natural disaster, the way they're always painted by philosophical film theorists.

Zombies are a human disaster.

Zombies could only have been come up with by self-centered assholes like us. Parakeets would never think of sick nonsense like this. They're too busy being pretty, eating bugs and not starting wars over stupid petty crap. Zombies are the cool, slick, awesome way that we destroy our planet, as opposed to the sad, slow, real one. They're the failure of culture. They're the failure of the self. And no one, from Pablo Picasso to Adolf Hitler, from Kurt Cobain to Alexander the Great, wants to live in a world where the failure of the self defines your daily existence.

I should've known not to use the time machine from the moment Gunther triggered the catalytic reaction. I didn't realize jumping backwards would create a global radioactive shockwave. I remember vividly the moment that I teleported back onto the location at Union Pacific Avenue in downtown Los Angeles. For a second everything was perfect, and then I realized the radiological impact of my having moved through time had instantly rendered three-quarters of the world's population mindless, their skin tinted green with scurvy, either eyes popped and sallow like burst balloons.

I will never forget Michael Jackson's screams as my father and Rick Baker ate him alive.

I always wanted to be famous. Ever since I was little, I wanted people to come up to me on the street the way they came up to my father. And now, they do. I move from city to city, hunting other survivors. It's very important to me that you read this. That someone reads it.

And that's why I staple it to the body of every fresh kill. People need to know the limits of their individuality. People need to know that the world wasn't always like this; that being yourself is beautiful, but being part of the human race is better.

That's why I have to keep killing, you see.

I have to make it less cool to be a survivor.

—Max Landis, 3/24/14

Illustrations by Ashley Perryman Quach

INTRODUCTION OF THE LIVING DEAD

There's been a shift in the natural order. Lumbering hordes of reanimated, rotting corpses are roaming the streets, seemingly with no purpose. But make no mistake, they are ferocious and they are relentless. They will chase, climb, pound, scratch, and crawl to feed on the living. These soulless automatons are not monsters from another realm, nor creatures from outer space. They are walking-dead men and women and even children. They are loved ones, friends, and neighbors who have returned from the grave with an insatiable appetite and a singular, irrational purpose—to devour your living human flesh. Try as you may to resist the onslaught, your attempts at survival will be futile, and you'll still be alive when they begin to consume you. But your inevitable demise will not end in a peaceful, eternal slumber. Rather, that's when the real nightmare begins, once you've succumbed to death—that's when you start to turn, when you lose any will of your own. That's when you transform into the very thing that frightens and fascinates you most of all: ZOMBIES ON FILM. Unlike vampires, ghosts, demons, werewolves, and even Frankenstein's monster, which all trace their lineage back hundreds of years to familiar literary works, gothic fairy tales, and classic mythological legends, our modern-day perception of zombie lore was created and defined in the twentieth century, at the movies.

Motion pictures have always been a predominantly commercial medium, the product of a somewhat paradoxical synthesis between commerce and art. While film producers and financiers traditionally choose what films to make based on reliable trends and bottom lines, the writers and directors they partner with are typically storytellers, and they have something to say. The most talented are able to craft economical yet commercially thrilling premises while making valuable social observations. It was at that precise alignment of commerce and artistry where the modern-day zombie was conceived. If necessity is the mother of all inventions, then George A. Romero is the father.

Romero's 1968 masterpiece, *Night of the Living Dead*, which he directed and co-wrote with John A. Russo on a shoestring budget, reset and revitalized the living dead canon without even referencing or uttering the word "zombie." Romero not only crafted a disturbingly fresh reimagination of that familiar and cost-effective trope, but also masterfully integrated a cautionary tale about society's inability to communicate and its subsequent disintegration. Those social themes, combined with Romero's nihilistic approach to the material, still affect audiences today. And although it took years to get recognized, the film's transcendent impact on popular culture was evident by the turn of the century, when the Library of Congress selected *Night of the Living Dead* for preservation in the National Film Registry as a motion picture deemed "culturally, historically, or aesthetically significant" to the United States.

Opposite: Cinema's first flesh-eating zombie (S. William Hinzman) attacks Johnny (Russell Streiner) and Barbara (Judith O'Dea) in George Romero's *Night of the Living Dead* (1968).

Below: Theatrical one-sheet for producer Val Lewton's 1943 thriller.

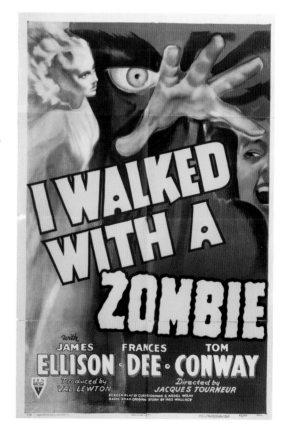

Above: Special makeup effects artist Greg Nicotero's ghoul from writer-director Frank Darabont's *The Walking Dead* (2010).

Below: George A. Romero on the set of *Diary of the Dead* (2007).

Opposite: Spanish one-sheet for a 1981 re-release of *Night of the Living Dead* (1968).

Prior to *Night of the Living Dead*, zombies had been almost exclusively derived from Haitian folklore, and were associated with voodoo cults and mind control, as depicted in *White Zombie* (1932). That film, considered to be the first feature-length zombie picture, starred Hungarian-born actor Bela Lugosi, best known for his memorable portrayal in Universal's horror classic *Dracula* (1931). However, since their motion picture debut, zombies have always struggled to maintain a respectable screen presence alongside Hollywood's classic A-list monsters. Producers generally resorted to zombies when searching for alternative low-cost antagonists to put in their horror flicks. For the most part, zombies are rights free, so no costly literary or intellectual rights need to be paid to use them. High-wage movie stars aren't needed to play them—the roles of the faceless zombie hordes usually go to lower-salaried extras. And zombies don't necessarily require extravagant prosthetics makeup effects or expensive costume builds. In fact, you could just get homeless itinerants to play your zombies, as director Lucio Fulci is rumored to have done for his spectacle of gore, *Zombie* (*Zombi 2* [1979]). Given those circumstances, the living dead have spent much of their cinematic history starring in obscure low-budget exploitation films. Fortunately, every so often, visionary filmmakers like Romero and Fulci emerge onto the scene, breathing new life into a stale, left-for-dead concept by delivering relevant and shocking experiences for audiences. It's this spirit of independent filmmaking that has made zombies thrive, and what has consistently carried them into new eras. This is how a legend is created.

By his own assertions, Romero was always partial to the traditional Caribbean zombie archetype seen in *White Zombie* (1932)—referring to them as "blue-collar monsters." Under the hypnotic spell of an evil voodoo master, these zombie minions did all the heavy lifting while their master rested comfortably in his castle. However, Romero's interpretation eliminated the voodoo master and transplanted the Caribbean-centric living dead concept to modern-day suburbia, refashioning them as regular working-class corpses—our neighbors, friends, and family. By making the threat relatable to audiences, the cinematic experience suddenly became more disturbing. The roots of those influences can also be found in author Richard Matheson's 1954 post-apocalyptic novel, *I Am Legend*, which Romero acknowledges was his greatest single inspiration in creating *Night of the Living Dead*. The premise centers on the last lone survivor of a pandemic plague that wiped out the rest of humanity by turning them into vampires. Released four years prior to *Night of the Living Dead*, the novel's film adaptation *The Last Man on Earth* (1964), starring Vincent Price in the titular role, was subsequently remade as *The Omega Man* (1971), with Charlton Heston, and *I Am Legend* (2007), starring Will Smith. Matheson's post-apocalyptic premise and diseased antagonists resonated

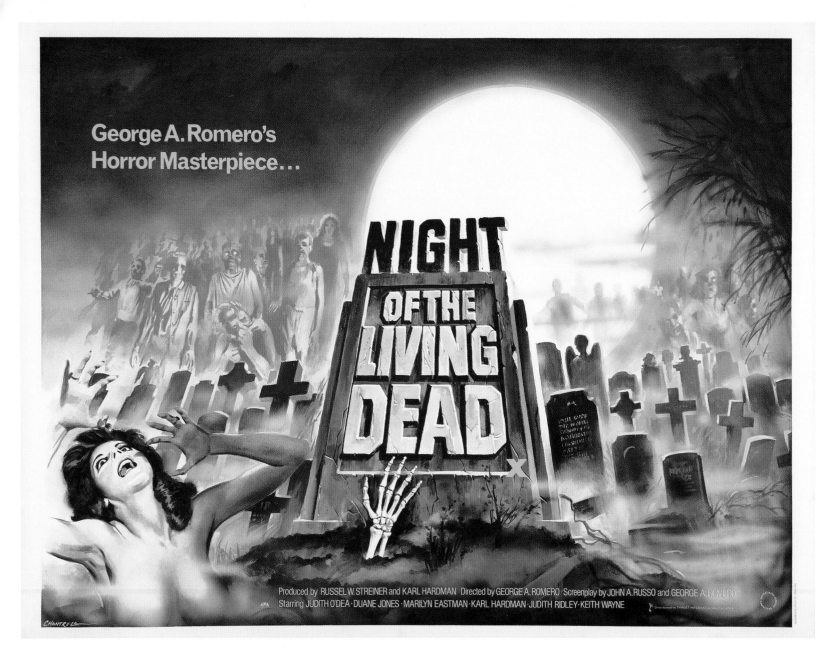

Opposite: A spooky British poster for a re-release (top); in *Warm Bodies* (2013) Julie (Teresa Palmer) compares Nicholas Hoult to director Lucio Fulci's flesh-eating progenitor (bottom).

with Romero, who wondered, if *I Am Legend* portrays mankind's revolutionary last days, what about the beginning of the end? How did those first last days unfold? What if these are them? What if the creatures weren't vampires?

Discussing the value of cultural transfers, filmmaker Francis Ford Coppola once invoked an essay by French novelist Honoré de Balzac about a young writer who stole some of his prose. "As for young writers taking what we're doing and copying it and letting that be a starting point—we ask you to do that. We're proud to be part of that link. We did it to those that came before us. So please steal from it, because you can't steal from it, because as you work it will become your own. And then someone will come and steal from that, and in that way we're alive forever." Coppola added, "I've always encouraged young artists to, at first when they're young, to take a piece and start to rip it off because that's how you will find your own voice or style . . . and that's good, that's what it's supposed to be. That's the cultural transfer that happens from generation to generation."

For over eighty years these ravenous cinematic corpses have been feeding, thriving, and evolving on the imaginations and creative works of a talented stable of writers, directors, producers, actors, illustrators, special makeup effects artists, and video-game designers. These stewards of storytelling have paid the legacy forward and left a lasting and indelible impression on the subgenre, one which the zombies will carry with them forever; whether they're pacing hypnotically to Lugosi in *White Zombie* (1932), terrorizing funnyman Bob Hope in *The Ghost Breakers* (1940), ratcheting up Cold War fears in *Invisible Invaders* (1957), ushering in an apocalyptic future in *Night of the Living Dead* (1968), raiding the temple to consumerism in *Dawn of the Dead* (1978), immersed in gruesome splatter in *Zombie* (1979), dancing along with Michael Jackson in *Thriller* (1983), craving brains in *Return of the Living Dead* (1985), storming the castle for laughs in *Army of Darkness* (1992), ravaging Raccoon City in *Resident Evil: Apocalypse* (2004), finding love in *Warm Bodies* (2013), or swarming the globe in *World War Z* (2013).

Above: A special makeup effects workstation for *The Walking Dead* (2010-).

Overleaf: An alien army of walking corpses marches in *Invisible Invaders* (1959).

WITH THESE ZOMBIE EYES
he rendered her powerless

WHITE ZOMBIE

WITH THIS ZOMBIE GRIP
he made her perform his every desire!

Printed in U.S.A.

HOLLYWOOD SUMMONS

THE DEAD

By 1930, talking pictures were heralding Hollywood's golden age, and horror films were emerging as a successful trend with cinemagoers. Studios were increasingly adapting renowned literary tales of the macabre, delivering terrifying chills and shocking thrills. The most notable hits at the start of the decade were Universal Pictures' adaptations of Bram Stoker's novel *Dracula* (1931), directed by Tod Browning and starring Bela Lugosi; Mary Shelley's *Frankenstein* (1931), directed by James Whale, starring Boris Karloff; and Paramount Pictures' retelling of Robert Louis Stevenson's *Dr. Jekyll and Mr. Hyde* (1931), under the direction of Rouben Mamoulian, and starring Fredric March. These early talkies set the standard for American horror, and their success at the box office launched a slate of horror films that extended well beyond the decade.

For Edward and Victor Halperin, two brothers from Chicago who had found moderate success in Hollywood producing romantic melodramas for the major studios of the Silent Era—Victor would direct, Edward would produce—making talkies during the Great Depression proved challenging. But they recognized the public's growing interest in the horror genre, and decided to embark on an original property that would exploit America's newfound curiosity in voodoo lore. The idea for the Halperin Brothers' new film originated from the pages of William Seabrook's 1929 nonfiction travelogue about his exotic adventures in Haiti, *The Magic Island*. It recounted dark tales of native voodoo rites that essentially brought the dead back to life as zombies. But Seabrook's shocking first-person accounts were extraordinary, and nothing like the miraculous narratives Westerners had been familiar with, such as Jesus Christ's divine resurrection of Lazarus as depicted in the Holy Bible's Gospel of John. Zombies were reanimated corpses without souls, bodies without any physical liberty or personal autonomy. They existed at the mercy of voodoo sorcerers and functioned as servile labor. Seabrook's lurid encounters challenged science and defied religion, so naturally the public was captivated.

The Halperin Brothers seized their inspiration and commissioned writer Garnett Weston to develop and write an original concept and screenplay for what would become the zombie's feature film debut—*White Zombie* (1932). The eerie melodrama follows blonde Madeline Short (Madge Bellamy) to Haiti to marry her dashing fiancé Neil Parker (John Harron). In order to prevent the marriage, Madeline's secret admirer, Charles Beaumont (Robert Frazer) invites the couple to stay at his tropical mansion and offers to host their wedding. Unable to win her devotion through traditional means, Beaumont seeks the assistance of a malevolent necromancer who turns Madeline into a zombie. That sinister role went to "Bela

Opposite: Theatrical one-sheet for *White Zombie* (1932).

Below: Advertising art from Universal's *Dracula* (1931).

Above: Bela Lugosi's Murder Legendre in *White Zombie* was enhanced by special makeup effects artist Jack P. Pierce.

Opposite: *White Zombie*'s art director Ralph Berger repurposed portions of the set pieces from Castle Dracula's great hall and staircase (top) for Legendre's (Lugosi) Haitian castle (bottom).

Overleaf: The zombies in *White Zombie* were created by master Hollywood special makeup-effects legend Jack P. Pierce.

(Dracula) Lugosi," whom the Halperins managed to secure for a nominal fee one year after his breakout success playing Universal's bloodsucking count.

Lugosi plays the aptly named Murder Legendre with evil aplomb. His devilish widow's peak, downturned mustache, pitchfork goatee, and dastardly upturned eyebrows were created by master Hollywood makeup artist Jack P. Pierce. Pierce also fashioned cinema's first zombies into pale living-dead gargoyles. Each was an individual character with a distinct look and wardrobe. Applying dark makeup to the hollow areas of each performer's face enhanced bony features and bugged-out eyes. Pierce was the notable head of Universal's makeup department, and on loan to the Halperins for the production. Known for creating Boris Karloff's character-defining look as the monster in *Frankenstein*, he also fashioned the classic makeup designs for *The Mummy* (1932), *The Black Cat* (1934), *Bride of Frankenstein* (1935), and *The Wolf Man* (1941). An innovator in the field, Pierce's enduring work went on to influence generations of future special makeup effects artists like Rick Baker, Tom Savini, and Greg Nicotero.

White Zombie was reportedly shot in just eleven days, mostly on the Universal studio lot in Southern California, for under $75,000—a paltry sum compared to the scale of Universal's *Dracula* (estimated at $341,191) and *Frankenstein* (estimated at $291,129). Although the zombie's first cinematic outing was independently bankrolled by a motion-picture financing firm out of New York and not a major studio, the Halperin Brothers' years of experience had shaped them into savvy and resourceful moviemakers, so they managed to achieve high production values with studio-level quality for a fraction of the cost. Their art director, Ralph Berger, a veteran of movie serials, rented and expertly repurposed preexisting set pieces and scenery from the epic horror films of the era. Berger rearranged the pillars and hanging balcony set from *The Hunchback of Notre Dame* (1923), the dark corridors used in *Frankenstein*, and Castle Dracula's great hall and staircase for Murder Legendre's Haitian castle. Technically, Lugosi was back home, but the audience wouldn't recognize it. Like Dr. Frankenstein piecing together various human body parts to create a new man, the Halperins and their crew used Hollywood parts to craft a new kind of story, and gave birth to a new type of monster.

Director of photography Arthur Martinelli made the most of the set pieces by composing objects in the foreground to create depth within the frame and gave the film a dark, atmospheric look by incorporating ominous shadows throughout

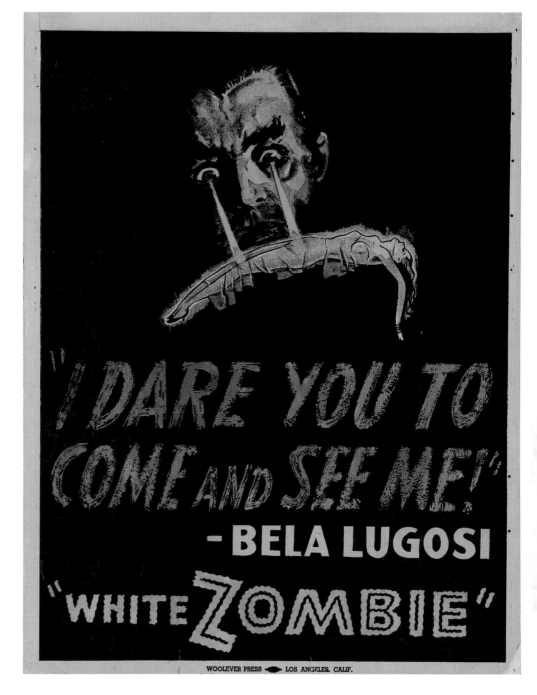

the sets. The most menacing and iconic image in *White Zombie* became the extreme close-up of Lugosi's hypnotic eyes as Legendre exerts his will over his zombies—they fill the frame and break the fourth wall. To achieve this, Martinelli cut two holes out of a cardboard sheet and then placed it over Lugosi's face, spot lighting just his eyes, which gave them an ominous glow. Lugosi's trance worked on audiences, too, as the film proved to be immensely successful at the box office. Released through United Artists on July 28, 1932, *White Zombie* reportedly earned $1.7 million dollars at the box office. In comparison, by June of 1932, *Dracula* and *Frankenstein* had made $1.2 million and $1.4 million, respectively.

"DO YOU BELIEVE IN ZOMBIES?" asked a 1932 United Artists publicity handbill given out to theater managers. Just as Seabrook was evasive about the zombie's actual existence in *The Magic Island*, so was the film, which claimed, "Wherever there's superstition, you will also find fact." *Time* magazine's August 1932 review gave a vague explanation, further perpetuating the mystery among the public: "Voodoo is still esoterically practiced in Haiti. The Penal Code, Article 249, reads: 'If, after the administration of such substances [drugs to induce a coma-like death] the person has been buried, the act shall be considered murder, no matter what result follows.' No scientist has investigated zombies. But reports indicate that the term means people who have died of disease, old age or wounds and, before decomposition, been reanimated."

Most reviewers were unkind to *White Zombie*. The *New York Times* even used one of the film's lines in its critique, "Better death than that." Despite the reviews, audiences were captivated, and the movie was successfully re-released throughout the 1930s. But as the decade wore on and the public's perceptions and expectations of horror evolved, the film's style and silent-movie influences proved less terrifying to newer audiences. The Halperins' picture had decidedly laid the groundwork for future zombies on film, and many independent producers aspired to duplicate its low budget and high-return success. But the major Hollywood studios didn't attribute the film's box-office prosperity solely to the Caribbean voodoo concept. Rather, they saw *White Zombie* as merely a zombie variant of Bela

Above: A late 1930s window card promoting the film's re-release.

Opposite: Lobby cards for the original 1932 release of *White Zombie* feature Bela Lugosi, Madge Bellamy, and Robert Frazer.

Lugosi's *Dracula*. As such, Boris Karloff's popular roles in *Frankenstein* and *The Mummy* could also be repurposed and repackaged as living dead concepts.

In the British-produced film *The Ghoul* (1933), Karloff stars as dying Professor Morlant, an eccentric Egyptologist who insists on being entombed with the "Eternal Light" gemstone—a mystical jewel that will bring him eternal life. But when Morlant dies, the jewel is stolen, and he returns as a gaunt, walking-dead brute with bushy gray eyebrows to wreak his vengeance on those that double-crossed him, albeit with a twist ending. Although the film proved more popular with UK audiences than with their American counterparts, Warner Bros. was undeterred from resuscitating Karloff yet again for their own picture. In fact, they scored big with their first foray into the living dead subgenre. From an original story by Ewart Adamson and Joseph Fields, *The Walking Dead* (1936) was developed at Warner Bros. as a starring vehicle for Karloff, and it remains his most popular non-Universal horror title. The studio's legendary director Michael Curtiz (*Captain Blood* [1935], *Casablanca* [1942]) melds a hauntingly moving horror picture with religious overtones and the gangster melodramatics Warner Bros. was known for at the time. Dr. Beaumont (Edmund Gwenn), an admirable scientist curious to learn the mysteries of the afterlife, retrieves the body of John Ellman (Karloff), a sympathetic musician executed by the state for a crime he did not commit. Through the miracle of science, in a laboratory sequence echoing *Frankenstein*, Beaumont manages to revive Ellman's body.

Just prior to principal photography, Karloff successfully lobbied to adjust some of the scripted attributes of his living dead persona, such as tempering his physical agility, which he felt would produce unwanted laughter, and endowing him with some limited speech to differentiate the character from his role in *Frankenstein*. Karloff's walking dead is heartbreaking and chilling, a soulless portrayal of Ellman's former self—gaunt with a prominent white streak of hair and partial paralysis that evokes a recovering stroke victim instead of a clichéd lumbering monster. Like an apparition seeking justice, he takes no vengeful actions against the racketeers who framed him; instead he unnerves them with his very presence and mournful stare. Their guilt and terror is what eventually brings about their violent demise.

It had been a few years since the word "zombie" was splashed across a movie theater marquee when Edward and Victor Halperin returned with their low-budget production of *Revolt of the Zombies* (1936). Although it was initially announced

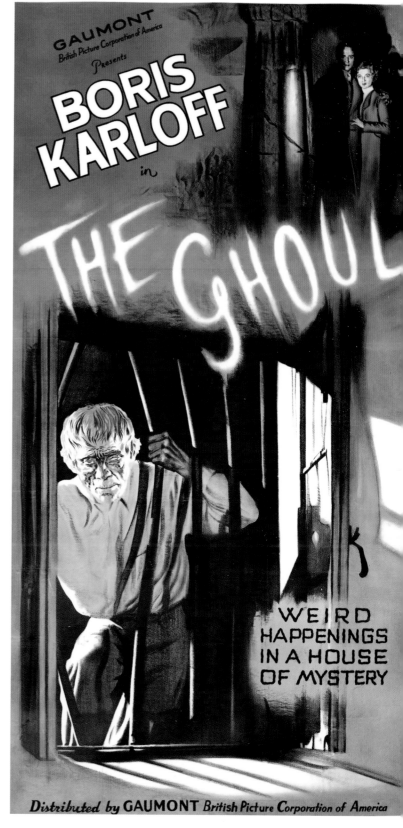

Above: A poster for *The Ghoul* may have been inspired by Karloff's other shuffling outing as *The Mummy* (1932).

Overleaf: Karloff returned from the dead again in director Michael Curtiz's *The Walking Dead* (1936).

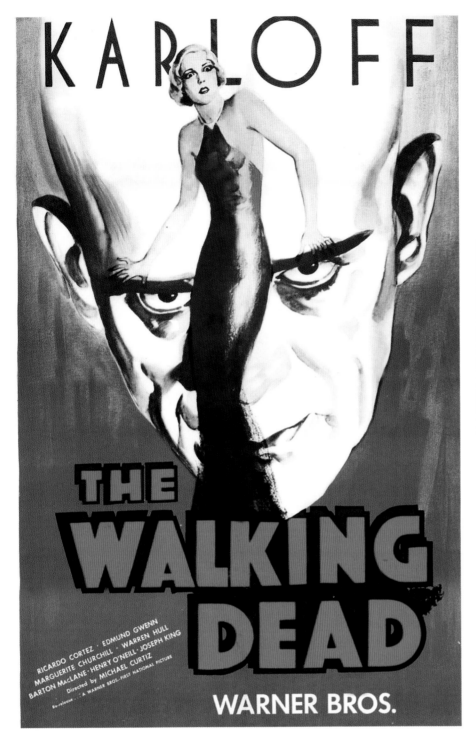

This page: Theatrical one-sheet (top left); John Ellman (Karloff) is revived in Dr. Beaumont's (Edmund Gwenn) lab (top right); Karloff's heartbreaking portrayal of the revived musician echoes a recovering stroke victim rather than a lumbering monster (bottom).

in the Hollywood trade publications as a sequel to *White Zombie*, the finished picture appears to have only one direct link other than the word "zombie." Bela Lugosi's hypnotic glowing eyes from the original film were shamelessly recycled, superimposed over the new picture's zombie trance sequences– a wistful reminder of how much Lugosi's star presence is missed in this outing. Regardless, the Halperins were treading new ground with another original idea, prefaced in *Revolt of the Zombies'* tantalizing opening crawl: "Many strange events were recorded in the secret archives of the fighting nations during the world war . . . But none stranger than that which occurred when a regiment of French Cambodians from the vicinity of the lost city of Angkor arrived on the Franco-Austrian front." With this follow-up, the sibling filmmakers expanded the subgenre's scope by breaking their own rules. They unconventionally ditched the zombie's indigenous Haitian component that they had introduced in *White Zombie* and made these zombies native to Indo-China, so they could incorporate them onto the frontlines of World War I.

The story unfolds with General Duval (George Cleveland) of the French army learning about an invulnerable Cambodian regiment under the command of a mysterious priest. The Cambodian soldiers, able to slaughter enemy combatants and easily capture their trenches, are zombies! Worried that an army consisting of Cambodian zombie soldiers could be an unstoppable force against the "white race," General Duval commissions an archeological expedition to the ruins of Angkor Wat to find and destroy the source behind its power, the "Secret of the Zombies." But a Halperin Brothers' zombie picture would not be complete without romantic melodrama at its core. And in *Revolt of the Zombies*, the brothers lay it on thick, essentially reusing the same love-triangle plot from *White Zombie*. During the expedition, linguistics expert Armand Louque (Dean Jagger) falls head over heels in love with Claire (Dorothy Stone), the general's daughter, but Claire has eyes for another man. When Armand stumbles upon the "Secret of the Zombies" inside an ancient temple, he uses his newfound mind-control powers to create his own zombie army that holds claim over all of Cambodia, and then blackmails Claire into marrying him. While the war setting and themes of world domination were timely and prescient metaphors in 1936, the picture's inferior execution made it incapable of matching the aesthetic or financial success of *White Zombie,* when the Halperins had first introduced movie audiences to a chilling new subgenre.

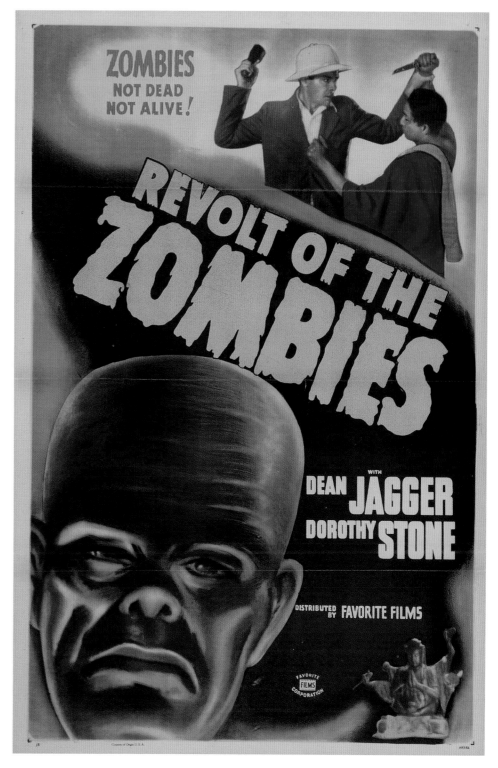

Above: Theatrical one-sheet for the Halperin Brothers' low-budget 1936 sequel to their hit *White Zombie.*

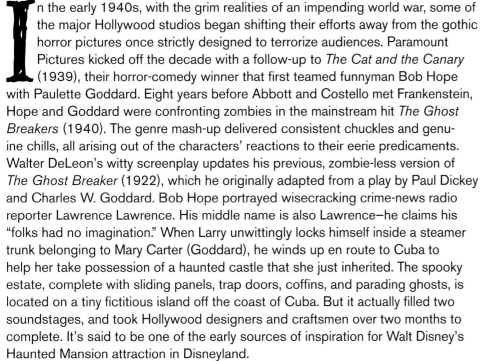

RISING OUT OF POVERTY ROW

In the early 1940s, with the grim realities of an impending world war, some of the major Hollywood studios began shifting their efforts away from the gothic horror pictures once strictly designed to terrorize audiences. Paramount Pictures kicked off the decade with a follow-up to *The Cat and the Canary* (1939), their horror-comedy winner that first teamed funnyman Bob Hope with Paulette Goddard. Eight years before Abbott and Costello met Frankenstein, Hope and Goddard were confronting zombies in the mainstream hit *The Ghost Breakers* (1940). The genre mash-up delivered consistent chuckles and genuine chills, all arising out of the characters' reactions to their eerie predicaments. Walter DeLeon's witty screenplay updates his previous, zombie-less version of *The Ghost Breaker* (1922), which he originally adapted from a play by Paul Dickey and Charles W. Goddard. Bob Hope portrayed wisecracking crime-news radio reporter Lawrence Lawrence. His middle name is also Lawrence—he claims his "folks had no imagination." When Larry unwittingly locks himself inside a steamer trunk belonging to Mary Carter (Goddard), he winds up en route to Cuba to help her take possession of a haunted castle that she just inherited. The spooky estate, complete with sliding panels, trap doors, coffins, and parading ghosts, is located on a tiny fictitious island off the coast of Cuba. But it actually filled two soundstages, and took Hollywood designers and craftsmen over two months to complete. It's said to be one of the early sources of inspiration for Walt Disney's Haunted Mansion attraction in Disneyland.

Joined by Larry's black valet, Alex (Willie Best), our heroes encounter more than just voodoo threats, gun-toting bad guys, and phantoms. The creaky castle is also haunted by the memorably terrifying Zombie (Noble Johnson), and his "Ma'" (Virginia Brissac). "I was really frightened," Goddard later claimed. "I never suffered from insomnia in my life, until I saw that zombie in my dreams." This film's walking menace stands over six feet tall, and contrary to previous zombies on film, it is made up to actually look like a rotting corpse with mottled, decomposing flesh and tattered garments. Johnson's impressive physique made the character monstrous, towering over the other actors. Besides being a noted performer, Johnson, whose acting career spanned the Silent Era, and later played memorable roles as the Nubian in *The Mummy* (1932) and as Skull Island's Native Chief in *King Kong* (1933), was also one of America's black film industry pioneers. He co-founded the Lincoln Motion Picture Company with his brother in 1915, expressly producing narrative feature films that portrayed blacks in America with dignity. Hollywood films of the period were notorious for depicting black Americans as demeaning caricatures, consistently typecasting them as the help, whose slang and wide-eyed expressions were played up for punch lines. In fact, *The Ghost Breakers* perpetuates some of these black stereotypes with Willie Best's quaking sidekick, Alex.

Opposite: Noble Johnson's menacing Zombie wards off intruders in *The Ghost Breakers* (1940).

Below: Bob Hope and Paulette Goddard in *The Ghost Breakers*.

Above: Larry Lawrence (Hope) and his trusty valet, Alex (Willie Best), in *The Ghost Breakers*.

Opposite: Before Johnson played the monstrous Zombie in *The Ghost Breakers*, he was one of America's black film industry pioneers.

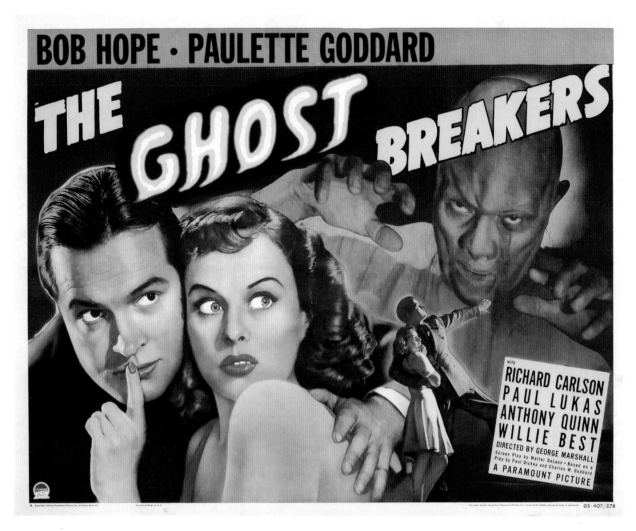

Above: Poster for the hit 1940 horror-comedy mash-up.

Opposite: Dean Martin and Jerry Lewis took over for Hope and Best in *Scared Stiff* (1953), the successful remake of *The Ghost Breakers.*

Pages 42-43: Theatrical one-sheet and lobby cards for Monogram's *King of the Zombies* (1941).

However, the result is comparatively tempered due mostly to Bob Hope, whose cowardly presence deflects some of the laughs from falling solely on Best—who saves the day in the end. According to the *Hollywood Reporter*'s review at the time, director George Marshall utilized Best's talents to great comedic effect. "For his management of this character alone, Marshall's direction shows penetrating comic insight. A colored man facing ghosts just about leads the lot of movie clichés, but as Marshall does it with Willie Best, it has the freshness of a new joke." Other critics at the time gave the unique horror-comedy points for its tone. *Variety* reported, "Its lightness and levity throughout, in these times of war, provide added impetus to bright biz prospects." And they were right; *The Ghost Breakers* was a resounding success with audiences, so much so that Paramount and Marshall reunited thirteen years later for another successful remake—*Scared Stiff* (1953), with Dean Martin replacing Hope and comedian Jerry Lewis stepping in for Best.

Although zombies played a memorable and effective role in *The Ghost Breakers*, they wouldn't be seen again in mainstream studio fare for decades to come. Instead, a lower-tier class of independent studios, known for making cheap genre features, came calling. Nicknamed "Poverty Row," these B-movie studios such as Monogram Pictures welcomed the extant zombie concept and capitalized on its low-budget, big-screen potential. But the resulting films perpetually branded the zombie as a mediocre, low-rent movie monster. On the heels of *The Ghost Breakers*, Monogram put out a successive slate of zombie-themed films including *King of the Zombies* (1941), *Bowery at Midnight* (1942), *Revenge of the Zombies* (1943), and *Voodoo Man* (1944). *King of the Zombies*' makers imitated *The Ghost Breakers*' formula by combining horror and comedy and pairing a white lead with a black sidekick. Actor Mantan Moreland was cast in the valet role, but without a lead like Bob Hope to balance out the humor, Moreland's character devolves into the caricature of the scaredy-cat foil he became famous for playing.

Any voodoo mumbo-jumbo rituals that justified *King of the Zombies'* remote island setting were nowhere to be found in its loose sequel, *Revenge of the*

10019-B

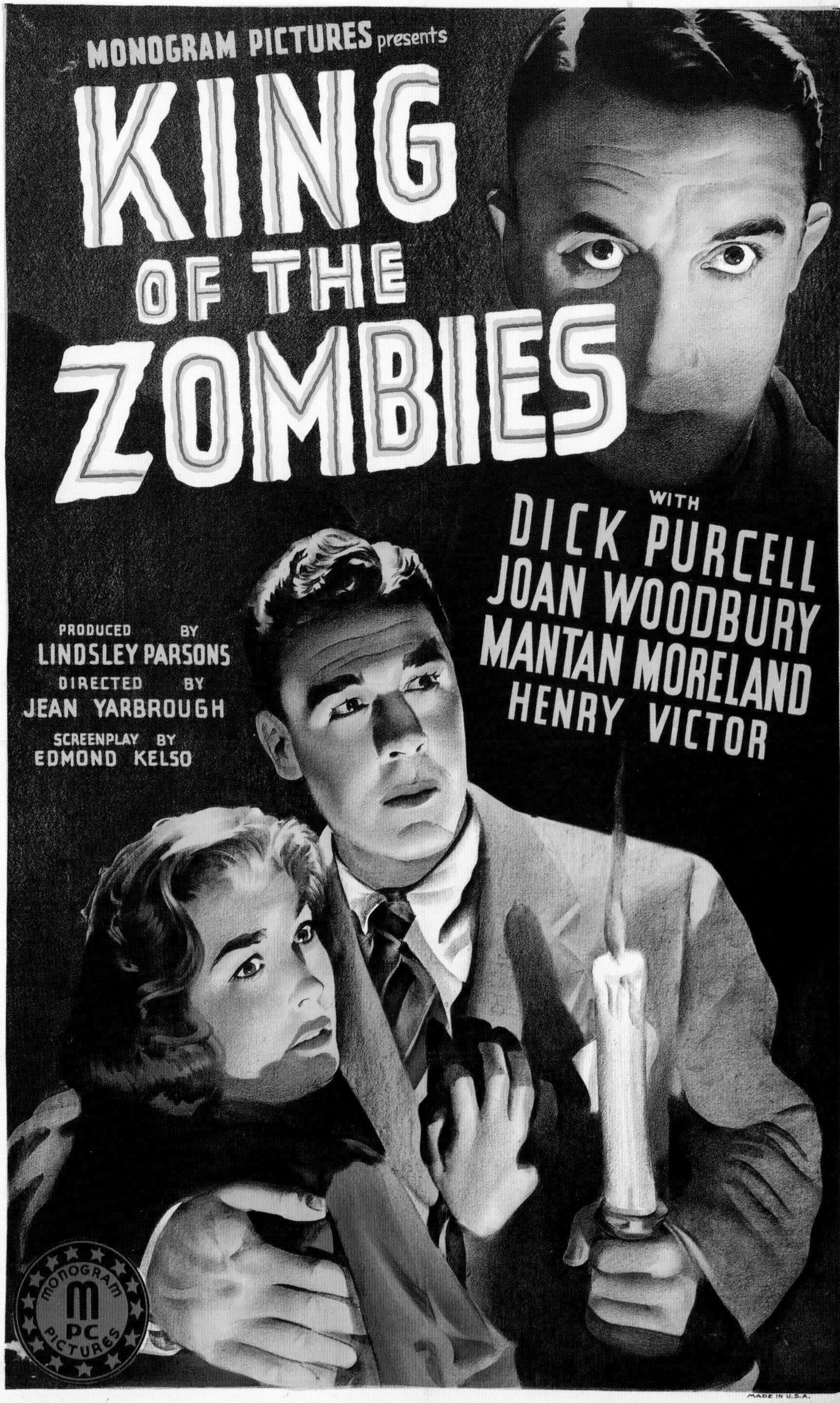
MONOGRAM PICTURES presents
KING OF THE ZOMBIES
WITH
DICK PURCELL
JOAN WOODBURY
MANTAN MORELAND
HENRY VICTOR
PRODUCED BY
LINDSLEY PARSONS
DIRECTED BY
JEAN YARBROUGH
SCREENPLAY BY
EDMOND KELSO
MONOGRAM M PC PICTURES
MADE IN U.S.A.

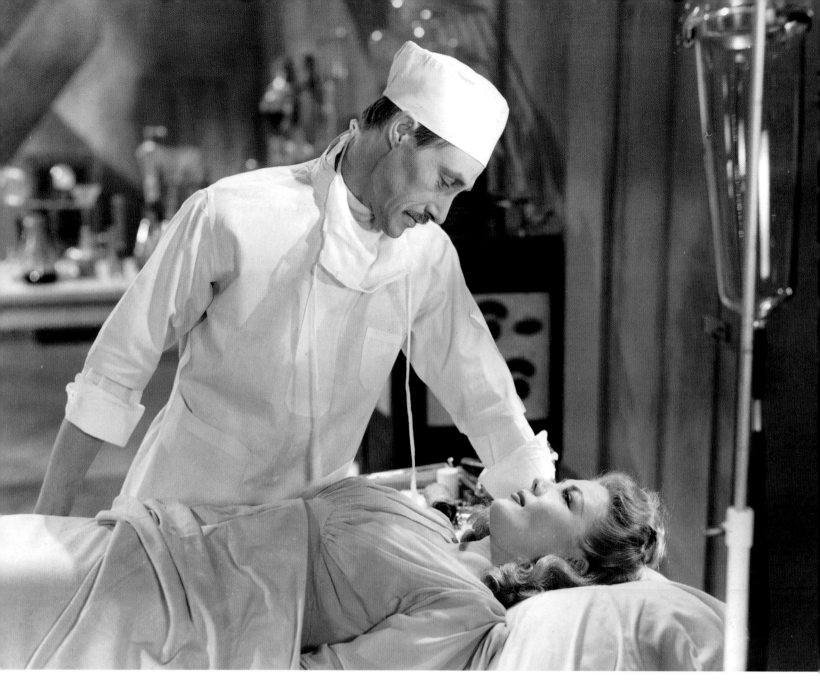

Above: Nazi doctor Von Altermann's (John Carradine) dreams of building an indestructible zombie army begining with reviving his wife Lila (Veda Ann Borg) in *Revenge of the Zombies* (1943).

Right: *Revenge of the Zombies* also starred Mantan Moreland, a talented performer usually relegated to playing the scaredy-cat foil.

Opposite: Half-sheet for Monogram's 1943 follow-up to *King of the Zombies*.

Zombies, which unfolds in the Louisiana bayou and employs science to bring back its dead. Despite their necromantic incongruence, both films have almost identical premises, yet *Revenge* drops the intentional comedy. Echoing similar themes from the Halperin Brothers' *Revolt of the Zombies*, it involves a scheming mad doctor who utilizes zombies to advance the national interests of his sinister foreign government, namely Germany. No doubt blatantly tailored for World War II audiences, the villainous Nazi doctor Von Altermann (John Carradine) boasts: "I am prepared to supply my country with a new army, numbering as many thousands as are required. An army that will not need to be fed . . . It cannot be stopped by bullets . . . That is in fact, invincible . . . An army of the living dead . . . Against an army of zombies, no armies could stand!" But apparently Monogram couldn't even afford ghoulish makeup for their zombie actors, forsaking any chance they had to appear menacing on camera.

Monogram's *Bowery at Midnight* (1942) and *Voodoo Man* (1944) are domestic-centric screen entries that heralded the return of Bela Lugosi to the zombie subgenre. But, regrettably, both the actor and the zombies are impaired by inferior material. *Bowery* is mostly a gangster crime caper that seems to be shamelessly employing the living dead concept as a marketing ploy. The film's absurd premise centers on Frederick Brenner (Lugosi), a professor of criminal psychology who secretly runs a soup kitchen in the Bowery area as a front for his criminal enterprise. Lugosi's character, a two-faced fiend, has a penchant for burying his murdered henchmen in the basement. But ultimately, he meets his own doom when his

MONOGRAM PICTURES Presents

BELA LUGOSI

BOWERY AT MIDNIGHT

with JOHN ARCHER · WANDA McKAY

PRODUCED BY SAM KATZMAN AND JACK DIETZ
DIRECTED BY WALLACE FOX
ORIGINAL SCREENPLAY BY GERALD SCHNITZER

LITHO. IN USA

Above and Right: Bela Lugosi administered his necromantic stare to the proceedings in *Voodoo Man* (1944).

Opposite: Theatrical one-sheet for Monogram's gangster-zombie hybrid *Bowery at Midnight* (1942).

BELA LUGOSI in "VOODOO MAN"

featuring
JOHN CARRADINE
GEORGE ZUCCO

A MONOGRAM PICTURE

Produced by SAM KATZMAN and JACK DIETZ
Associate Producer, BARNEY A. SARECKY
Directed by WILLIAM BEAUDINE
Original Story and Screenplay by ROBERT CHARLES

mad-doctor associate unexpectedly reanimates the vengeful corpses and sets them loose upon him. In *Voodoo Man* (1944), which unfolds in the dusty outskirts of Los Angeles, Lugosi plays Dr. Marlowe, a Vandyke-bearded eccentric who kidnaps and imprisons young girls. Using silly voodoo incantations and hypnosis, he then attempts to transfer their essence to his zombified wife, who's been dead for twenty-two years. The camera's extreme close-up of Lugosi's eyes as he hypnotizes his beautiful young victims recalls the actor's prime as voodoo-master Murder Legendre from *White Zombie* (1932).

In 1942, rival studio RKO Pictures hired Val Lewton, a writer and associate of legendary film producer David O. Selznick (*Gone with the Wind* [1939]) to head their new low-budget horror unit. Despite their low-budget trappings, Lewton believed that B movies could transcend their bargain-basement notoriety if they were infused with sophistication, style, and substance. RKO did give him a few provisos: budgets needed to remain under $150,000; running times needed to remain under seventy-five minutes; and the title would be determined by the studio, based on market testing. Lewton is said to have told his unit, "They may think I'm going to do the usual chiller stuff which will make a quick profit, be laughed at and forgotten, but I'm going to make the kind of suspense movies I like." But when the studio assigned him the title *I Walked with a Zombie* (1943), Lewton went home understandably glum. In fact, the studio had even already assigned scriptwriter Curt Siodmak, whose horror credits included Universal monster-movie fare like *The Wolf Man* (1941) and *The Ghost of Frankenstein* (1942). Lewton once quipped, "Actually, it's very difficult for a reviewer to give something called *I Walked with a Zombie* a good review." But by the next morning, Lewton, apparently having had a late-night revelation, announced to his team that they would be producing a "West Indian version of *Jane Eyre*." Together with his unit and director Jacques Tourneur, Lewton produced an eerie, sophisticated zombie picture that unleashes the genre's true cinematic potential by grounding the horror concept in a rationally convincing psychological thriller. And they shot it in three and a half weeks for $134,000. Lewton was involved not only in developing and writing the script; he shaped every aspect of the production and

JAMES ELLISON • FRANCES DEE • TOM CONWAY

IN I WALKED WITH A ZOMBIE

the blackest magic of voodoo keeps this beautiful woman alive... yet DEAD!

PRODUCED BY VAL LEWTON • DIRECTED BY JACQUES TOURNEUR • SCREEN PLAY BY CURT SIODMAK AND ARDEL WRAY
BASED ON AN ORIGINAL STORY BY INEZ WALLACE

Re-released by
R K O
RADIO

Above: Betsy Connell (Frances Dee) awakens a family's dark secrets in *I Walked with a Zombie.*

Left: The Canadian nurse (Dee) is summoned to the West Indies by a plantation owner (Tom Conway) to care for his catatonic wife Jessica (Christine Gordon).

Opposite: Jessica (Gordon) has been stricken by an unusual ailment.

She's **ALIVE**... YET DEAD!!!

She's **DEAD**... YET ALIVE!!!

Doomed to be one of the "walking dead" by weird and wily witchcraft...her radiant blonde loveliness ravaged through the curse of vengeful voodoo!

I walked with a ZOMBIE

with

JAMES ELLISON · FRANCES DEE · TOM CONWAY

Produced by VAL LEWTON · Directed by JACQUES TOURNEUR

SCREEN PLAY BY CURT SIODMAK AND ARDEL WRAY
BASED ON AN ORIGINAL STORY BY INEZ WALLACE

nt 1943 RKO Radio Pictures Inc.   Country of Origin U.S.A.

obsessed over every detail, all rooted in quality storytelling. An ardent researcher, in preparation he studied every book he could find on Haitian voodoo and even cast authentic voodoo musicians. Set on the fictitious island of San Sebastian in the West Indies, the movie shows a naïve Canadian nurse, played by Frances Dee, as she is summoned by a plantation owner to help care for his catatonic wife, who's been stricken with an unusual mental paralysis. When the nurse hears that local voodoo superstitions may be effective in curing her patient, she sets off in the darkness to find the tribal witchdoctor. Instead, she uncovers a disquieting family scandal and encounters a towering native zombie with glassy, protruding eyes named Carrefour (Darby Jones).

Lewton's efforts yielded the film mostly unanimous praise and became RKO's top moneymaker that year, earning nearly $4 million. The studio followed up the success with a loose sequel, but one not associated with Lewton and director Torneur. It's as if RKO was determined to produce their sensational B movie after all. A farcical departure from Lewton's atmospheric storytelling, *Zombies on Broadway* (1945) is a spoof about two screwball press agents, played by Wally Brown and Alan Carney, who head off to the island of San Sebastian in search of a real zombie for the opening of a New York night club called "The Zombie Hut." The always-dependable Bela Lugosi cameos as the evil professor who tries to thwart their antics by turning them into zombies, with the aid of the towering native Darby Jones, reprising his big-eyed walking-dead persona from *I Walked with a Zombie*. The picture was a hit for RKO, but a step back again to second-tier notoriety for the perambulating zombies.

Above: Lobby card for producer Val Lewton's original 1943 release.

Opposite: A late-night excursion into voodoo territory (top) where the nurse and her patient encounter the towering zombie, Carrefour (Darby Jones) (bottom) in director Jacques Tourneur's *I Walked with a Zombie* .

Above: Half-sheet for RKO's zany 1945 follow-up to *I Walked with a Zombie.*

Left: Bela Lugosi turns up as a mad doctor in *Zombies on Broadway* (1945).

Opposite: Inept press agents Mike Strager (Alan Carney) and Jerry Miles (Wally Brown) encounter Jean La Danse (Anne Jeffreys) in *Zombies on Broadway* (top). Their hunt for native zombies in San Sebastian leads to a transformative experience (bottom).

3 INVADERS FROM THE GRAVE!

The 1950s initiated a pivotal transitional period in the evolutionary development of the zombie subgenre. "Horror pictures are expressions of our time. During the Second World War, I wrote so-called gothic horror stories," recalled screenwriter Curt Siodmak (*The Wolf Man* [1941], *I Walked with a Zombie* [1943]). "When the war stopped, we couldn't sell these pictures anymore because there was a short time of peace. Then the atom bomb came and the horror pictures again became very prominent." A confluence of contemporary issues, from advancements in nuclear technology and early space exploration to an increased fear of Communism began affecting the national psyche. Horror films based on gothic literature or old folklore began to lose their significance, and a new kind of horror picture emerged out of the modern radioactive anxieties of the era, forgoing supernatural scares in favor of science fiction ones. Monster movies bred massive atomic creatures that wreaked large-scale havoc and laid waste to entire cities in *The Beast from 20,000 Fathoms* (1953), *Them!* (1954), *It Came from Beneath the Sea* (1955), and from Japan, the king of the monsters: *Godzilla* (1954). Shuffling zombies, beckoned by superstitious voodoo incantations, were lackluster compared to the allure of witnessing radioactive behemoths tear up the big screen. But the dead would rise again, albeit with some slight atomic alterations—and even if it meant terrorizing the bottom half of a science fiction double feature.

In 1955, Columbia Pictures produced and distributed *Creature with the Atom Brain* (1955) as a companion feature to one of their monster movies, *It Came from Beneath the Sea*, a top box-office hit for them that year. Written by Curt Siodmak, *Creature with the Atom Brain* transplants the zombie's traditional voodoo lore with new hardware from the atomic age, supplanting arcane superstition with ludicrous science fiction. A deported gangster (Michael Granger) returns stateside to take revenge on the district attorney and the double-crossers who testified against him. To carry out his ruthless plans, he enlists the services of an elderly misguided scientist who has discovered how to reanimate corpses through atomic radiation. In lieu of gazing into Bela Lugosi's hypnotic eyes, these zombies take orders via remote control. Electrodes implanted in the unstoppable henchmen's brains allows them to transmit audio and video signals back to their mobster master, who dispatches his commands into a microphone and then watches the terror unfold via closed-circuit television from the comfort and safety of his lair. That's innovation!

The walking-dead hit men blend right into their urban setting, making them a bit more disturbing than some of cinema's previous native-island zombies. These middle-aged lumbering stiffs look like average Joes in pressed suits on first glance, but closer inspection reveals the frontal lobotomy scars, bags under their lifeless

Opposite: Theatrical one-sheet for a new kind of zombie chiller for the 1950s.

Overleaf: Screenwriter Curt Siodmak substitutes voodoo rituals with atomic power in *Creature with the Atom Brain* (1955).

Above: Karl "Killer" Davis plays a reanimated corpse in *Creature with the Atom Brain*, and an undead sailor revived by a supernatural curse in *Zombies of Mora Tau* (1957) (opposite).

Left: Military forces are called in to stop urban zombies in director Edward Cahn's *Creature with the Atom Brain*.

eyes, and bullet holes and gashes across their faces from their encounters with the living. As the procedural crime drama unfolds, police employ Geiger counters and gather radioactive blood samples from crime scenes to advance their investigation. But when the probe successfully narrows in on the criminal mastermind responsible, he unleashes his zombie minions on a terror spree across the city, destroying buildings and public transportation and precipitating a state of emergency by the governor: "Acts of sabotage well beyond the previously established scope of the zombies," as *Variety* keenly observed in their review.

Columbia Pictures took a decidedly opposite approach with their next double-bill entry, *Zombies of Mora Tau* (1957). Unfolding on the coast of Africa, the horror movie foregoes the sci-fi trimmings, seemingly intent on recapturing the exotic locales and supernatural curses from old voodoo-inspired fare. Heading the production were two veterans of the subgenre: Edward Cahn, who had directed *Creature with the Atom Brain*, and genre-schlock producer Sam Katzman, who had a hand in *Creature*, and also produced *Voodoo Man* (1944) at Monogram before joining Columbia. Despite sinking at the box office due to its lack of modernity, *Mora Tau* introduced some significant on-screen firsts to the subgenre, including a premise that centers on a group of cursed sailors turned zombies that walk the ocean floor, a perceptible antecedent to Disney's worldwide blockbuster *Pirates of the Caribbean: The Curse of the Black Pearl* (2003).

"In the darkness of an ancient world—On a shore that time has forgotten—There is a twilight zone between life and death. Here dwell those nameless creatures who are condemned to prowl the land eternally—THE WALKING DEAD." Those

Opposite: Condemned dead seaman (Karl Davis) guards a cursed treasure in *Zombies of Mora Tau.*

Right: Lobby cards for Jerry Warren's ultra-low-budget *Teenage Zombies* (1959).

cautionary opening titles set the scene for the arrival of attractive young college student Jan Peters (Autumn Russell), in Africa after a ten-year absence, visiting her widowed great-grandmother (Marjorie Eaton). That same evening, a motley crew of opportunists anchors offshore, searching for an ancient sunken treasure that is buried in a shipwreck. Before long, the out-of-towners are attacked by a slow-moving pack of local zombies clothed in nautical attire and garnished with strands of seaweed. The old woman warns the skeptical visitors that the walking dead were cursed former crewmen from a nineteenth-century trading ship. As she tells it, "The sailors discovered a temple with a golden cask full of uncut diamonds. They stole the cask. There was a fight, and ten of the sailors were presumed dead, the captain among them. The others returned to the ship with the cask. Then, surprisingly, the ten missing men appeared—something happened. The rest of the crew was slaughtered, and the ship scuttled in the bay." She implores, "They were dead then and they're dead now! But they're still guarding those cursed diamonds! . . . They have no morality, no free will. They'll kill anyone who tries to steal the diamonds!" Undeterred by her warnings, the greedy expedition continues forward with catastrophic results.

In several cinematic firsts, *Mora Tau*'s condemned walking dead act without the existence of a master ordering them around. They also have the inexplicable power to turn the living into zombies, as they do when they kidnap the wife of the head treasure hunter and turn her against him. Their susceptibility and fear of fire is also introduced, as the heroes use torches, candles, and flares to ward them off in multiple sequences. One particular scene toward the end of the film is especially prescient in the evolution of the subgenre: when the zombies besiege the crew on the ship, trapping them inside their barricaded cabin, the crew is forced to resolve their differences in order to survive.

During the 1950s, many genre films contained themes and narratives reflecting Cold War anxieties of the period, including the Korean War, the Communist takeover of China and Eastern Europe, and the Red Scare in the United States. These events incited fears of foreign infiltration, subversion, indoctrination, and invasion, all evoking dread about the ultimate destruction of a free society. They were ripe themes for Hollywood to tackle, some of which hit close to home. Hundreds of artists, actors, directors, and particularly screenwriters were blacklisted by movie studios for alleged Communist activities, and many were forced to operate under pseudonyms to be able to work—Bernard Gordon used the front "Raymond T. Marcus" when he wrote *Zombies of Mora Tau.*

Zombies proved not only to be an ideal metaphor to tap into the public's psychological Red Scare jitters, but continued to be a reliably inexpensive one as well. In the case of *Teenage Zombies* (1959), the term "zombie" was exclusively

Above: One-sheet for *Teenage Zombies*.

Opposite: Lobby cards from *Plan 9 from Outer Space* (1958) capture Vampira and Tor Johnson as undead foot soldiers controlled by a foreign menace.

Pages 66-67: Grave robbers from outer space raise the dead in filmmaker Edward D. Wood, Jr.'s cult classic *Plan 9 from Outer Space*. Pictured left to right: Vampira, Tor Johnson, Tom Mason (doubling for Bela Lugosi), and Criswell.

referring to victims subjected to a type of mind control that was politically motivated. The ultra-low-budget film was specifically designed by moviemaker Jerry Warren to cash in on the popularity of drive-in theaters. Evidenced by its inferior production quality, the film offers teenage audiences exactly what they needed to sit back in their parked cars and lock lips—an excuse. The movie centers on a group of young friends who unmistakably match the exact teen demographic the film is targeting. After some debate at the local soda fountain about how to spend their carefree day, the boys and their female companions head off on a small motorboat to check out a desolate island. They soon fall prisoner to an evil female scientist and her brute zombie henchman, who was described by a *Los Angeles Times* reviewer as looking "like Fidel Castro under heavy sedation." Soon the vixen's evil plans reveal her intentions to turn the United States into a land of mindless worker zombies (read Commies). Along with her treasonous adult co-conspirators, she plans to poison the country's water supply with her hypnotic chemical toxin, which she successfully tests on a random gorilla (man in suit) and the two kidnapped teen girls. Fortunately, the boys break free from their caged cell and save the day, with a little help from the zombie gorilla.

Also at the time, a string of bigger-budget alien-invasion films were fusing Cold War angst with popular space-age visuals, producing titles such as *The Day the Earth Stood Still* (1951), *Red Planet Mars* (1952), *Invaders from Mars* (1953), and *The War of the Worlds* (1953). But financially strapped B movies such as *Plan 9 from Outer Space* (1958), and *Invisible Invaders* (1959) modified the zombie concept further and added them into the sci-fi mix.

Plan 9 from Outer Space and *Invisible Invaders* introduced a distinctly unique interplanetary twist on the subgenre, presenting a new class of undead—reanimated foot soldiers controlled by alien invaders from outer space. With mankind's nuclear ambition posing a threat to the galaxy at large, extraterrestrial beings come to Earth and turn the dead against living in order to destroy human civilization—a premise conveyed more concisely in *Plan 9 from Outer Space*'s original title, *Grave Robbers from Outer Space*. Written, produced, and directed by Edward D. Wood, Jr., *Plan 9 from Outer Space* emerged from obscurity in

PLAN 9 FROM OUTER SPACE

with
BELA LUGOSI
VAMPIRA
LYLE TALBOT

A J. Edward Reynolds Production

Produced and Directed by
Edward D. Wood, Jr.

a DCA release

PLAN 9 FROM OUTER SPACE

with
BELA LUGOSI
VAMPIRA
LYLE TALBOT

A J. Edward Reynolds Production

Produced and Directed by
Edward D. Wood, Jr.

a DCA release

UNSPEAKABLE HORRORS FROM OUTER SPACE PARALYZE THE LIVING AND RESURRECT THE DEAD!
PLAN 9 FROM OUTER SPACE
with
BELA LUGOSI
VAMPIRA
LYLE TALBOT
A J. Edward Reynolds Production
Produced and Directed by
Edward D. Wood, Jr.
a DCA release

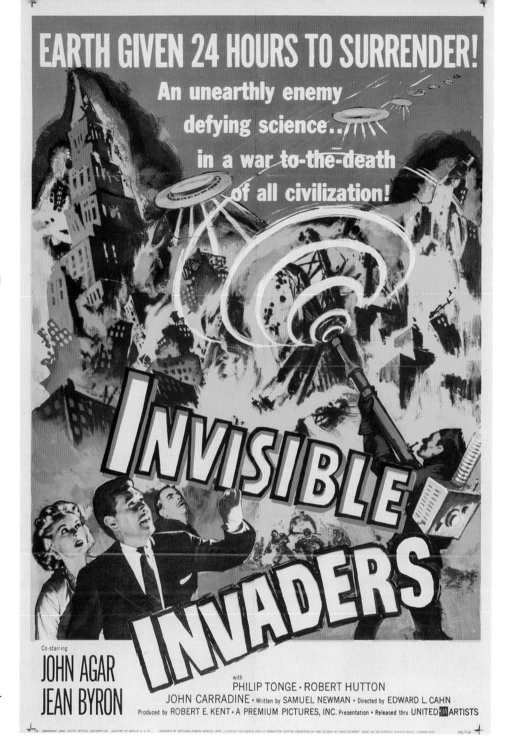

1980 when film critics Michael Medved and Harry Medved proclaimed it "the worst movie ever made." (Apparently neither of them had seen *Teenage Zombies*.) Wood was a passionate and imaginative filmmaker, characterized with blind optimism by actor Johnny Depp in producer-director Tim Burton's *Ed Wood* (1994). That film partly chronicles the making of *Plan 9 from Outer Space* and garnered actor Martin Landau an Academy Award for his portrayal of an elderly Bela Lugosi, whom Wood had befriended at the twilight of his career. Prior to Lugosi's death in 1956, the filmmaker shot footage of the actor pantomiming scenes for an unrelated project, even donning his iconic Dracula cape. Wood later incorporated the shelved footage into *Plan 9 from Outer Space* and credited Lugosi posthumously for the role of "Ghoul Man." Twenty-seven years after introducing the world to cinema's first zombie, Lugosi's last on-screen appearance would depict him as one.

Having previously helmed *Creature with the Atom Brain* and *Zombies of Mora Tau*, Edward Cahn once again returned to the subgenre to direct an alien army of walking corpses in *Invisible Invaders* (1959). These "invisible" spacemen with "invisible" spaceships were a surefire way of keeping production costs low. By inhabiting the bodies of dead earthlings, they manage to wreck havoc on a massive global scale—courtesy of generous amounts of bargain stock footage. Earth's only hope rests with four brave Americans: a military man, two scientists, and a blonde, holed up in a radioactive bunker and tasked by the government with finding a way to defeat the invaders. As hordes of walking dead dressed in their dusty burial suits and looking ashen descend outside the bunker, our heroes manage to work through their disagreements and stumble upon the spacemen's weakness—high-frequency sound.

What these B movies lacked in sophistication, due to their hokey executions, they made up for in concept. And although they didn't fully yet develop or capture a global zombie apocalypse on film, they ignited an idea only previously hinted at in *Revenge of the Zombies*. As one of the invisible invaders forewarns, "The dead will kill the living, and the people of earth will cease to exist." It was just a matter of time.

Above: *Invisible Invaders* (1959) infiltrate the deceased and bring mankind to its knees.

Opposite: Major Bruce Jay (John Agar) confronts an unstoppable army of corpses in *Invisible Invaders*.

4 ROMERO'S
REVOLUTION

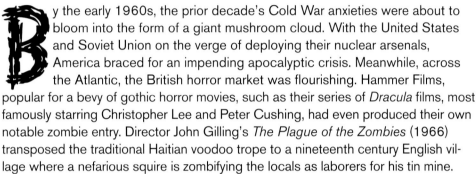

y the early 1960s, the prior decade's Cold War anxieties were about to bloom into the form of a giant mushroom cloud. With the United States and Soviet Union on the verge of deploying their nuclear arsenals, America braced for an impending apocalyptic crisis. Meanwhile, across the Atlantic, the British horror market was flourishing. Hammer Films, popular for a bevy of gothic horror movies, such as their series of *Dracula* films, most famously starring Christopher Lee and Peter Cushing, had even produced their own notable zombie entry. Director John Gilling's *The Plague of the Zombies* (1966) transposed the traditional Haitian voodoo trope to a nineteenth century English village where a nefarious squire is zombifying the locals as laborers for his tin mine.

Conversely, in America, Universal's gallery of famous monsters like Dracula, Frankenstein's monster, the Wolf Man, and the Mummy had lost their relevance, and with it their ability to frighten even children. In the shadow of the Cold War, classic monsters had become harmless and wholesome family fare, even satirized on the television sitcoms *The Munsters* (1964–66) and *The Addams Family* (1964–66), which aired in 1964 on CBS and ABC, respectively. That same year, film producer Robert Lippert and American International Pictures released the first feature-film adaptation of the chilling 1954 novel that would inspire a resurgence in the zombie subgenre, even though its creatures were technically vampires.

The Last Man on Earth (1964), based on Richard Matheson's acclaimed post-apocalyptic science fiction/horror novel *I Am Legend*, chronicles the tormented sole survivor of a pandemic plague that wipes out civilization, turning its victims into undead, bloodsucking vampires. Shot on a limited budget entirely in Italy and dubbed in English, the American-Italian coproduction stars Vincent Price, an actor primarily identified for the sinister cadence of his voice and camp debonair villainy. Here he's cast against type in the titular role, along with a supporting cast of mostly Italian actors, and under the direction of Sidney Salkow and Ubaldo Ragona. Esposizione Universale Roma, Benito Mussolini's unrealized pre–World War II modern Roman city, with its vacant buildings and empty streets, doubled for the film's post-apocalyptic nondescript American city.

Although it was remade years later starring Charlton Heston as *The Omega Man* (1971), and subsequently *I Am Legend* (2007), with Will Smith, *Last Man on Earth* is still considered to be the book's most faithful film adaptation. At the time, however, author Matheson, who had written the first draft of the script, was dissatisfied with the creative direction the project was taking and removed his name from the film. His alias "Logan Swanson" is credited, along with William Leicester. Pursuant to the novel, there is sophistication to the way the material is handled. The film has a grim, quiet tone that sets it apart from the campy clichés audiences had been accustomed to seeing in B movies. Even actor Price, who many felt was miscast, including Matheson, delivers a most restrained and straightforward performance.

Opposite: Theatrical one-sheet for *The Last Man on Earth* (1964) based on Richard Matheson's novel *I Am Legend*.

Below: Robert Morgan (Vincent Price) fends off undead friends and neighbors.

Overleaf: Barricaded inside his own home, earth's last known survivor (Price) makes distress calls with the hope someone is out there.

A large part of the story is told in flashbacks, as recurring nightmares that constantly torment Robert Morgan (Price), a scientist who was unable to find a cure for the disease that wiped out mankind, including his wife (Emma Danieli) and their infant daughter (Christi Courtland). As the plague spread globally, government and medical authorities were forced to take desperate measures, dumping the bodies of the infected into a fiery pit in an effort to reduce contagion. Although Morgan was unable to prevent his daughter from being incinerated in the pit, when his wife eventually succumbs to the affliction, he gives her a proper burial himself. But soon afterwards, her reanimated corpse returns home, ashen and caked in dirt, stumbling toward Morgan with her arms outstretched, hungry for his blood. Throughout the film, Morgan is harassed nightly by a lumbering mob of undead friends and neighbors, pounding on his barricaded windows and doors. "Morgan, come out. Come out!" they groan. While both the book and film refer to these walking dead as vampires—also evident by their aversion to garlic, crucifixes, mirrors, daylight, and death by stake through the heart, Matheson's unique take distances them beyond recognition from the traditional depictions Bela Lugosi made famous, so much so that they were repeatedly referred to as zombies in movie reviews, and even in the film's trailer. This bleak and pessimistic apocalyptic future, populated with infected living dead who mindlessly attack their surviving loved ones, would soon prove to have a significant and permanent impact on the future of zombies on film.

In 1967, a group of ten friends, most of whom operated a local production facility in Pittsburgh, Pennsylvania, that made television commercials and industrial films, pooled six hundred dollars each to form a new motion picture production company. It was called Image Ten, Inc., and although they hadn't yet chosen a story or a title, they decided that their first project would be a monster flick. At an eventual production cost of $114,000, it forever changed the nature of zombie movies, spawned a number of sequels and imitations, significantly influenced the horror genre, and was eventually selected by the United States Library

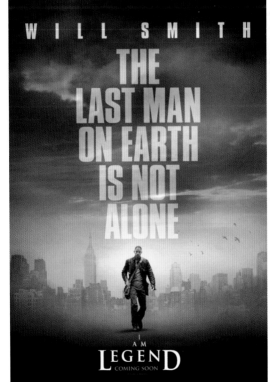

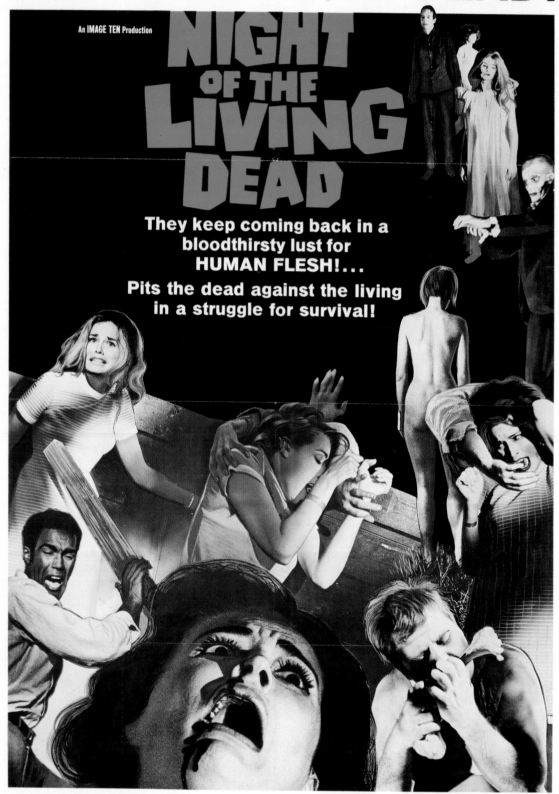

NO-14

of Congress for preservation in the National Film Registry. The first print of the completed film bore the title *Night of the Flesh Eaters*, but it would become internationally renowned by its amended title, *Night of the Living Dead* (1968).

"*I Am Legend* is loosely responsible for *Night of the Living Dead*," acknowledges the film's co-writer and director, George A. Romero. "Richard [Matheson] actually jokes with me saying that I stole his idea. And I keep saying, no, my guys aren't vampires!" The story genesis for *Night of the Living Dead* came from a short story Romero wrote and later adapted with co-writer John A. Russo into the screenplay. Although it was inspired by Matheson's post-apocalyptic novella, Romero made it his own, "*I Am Legend* is about . . . everyone in the world has become a vampire, and there's one guy left, and that's the last man on earth. I wanted to do something about, well, how did that start, and go back to the first night." Shot in 35mm Plus-X black-and-white stock, the landmark film fades in on a winding desolate road, following two teenagers as they pull their car into a remote cemetery. The siblings, Johnny (the film's producer, Russell Streiner) and Barbara (misspelled as "Barbra" in the closing credits, Judith O'Dea), are there to place a wreath on their father's grave, when, without provocation, they are randomly attacked by a mute transient. Johnny is knocked out cold, and Barbara flees. At first glance, the deranged man's ordinary appearance doesn't suggest he's a flesh-eating monster. But as he relentlessly pursues Barbara to a nearby farmhouse, his pasty complexion, stammering walk, and disheveled clothing begin to paint another picture. As Romero explained, "They certainly aren't vampires. They're not even zombies. Zombies for me were those boys in the Caribbean, who, you know, do the wetwork for Lugosi. I thought I was creating a completely new monster. You know, the neighbors that suddenly turn into flesh eaters, ghouls. That's what I called them, 'ghouls,' in the film. And I thought they were completely new." Contrary

Above: Flesh-eating ghouls emerge from the imagination of writer-director George A. Romero and make their debut in *Night of the Living Dead* (1968).

Opposite: Theatrical one-sheet for *Night of the Living Dead.*

Above: An idyllic farmhouse is besieged by hordes of ferocious corpses in *Night of the Living Dead* (1968).

Opposite: Ben (Duane Jones) fights off the hungry zombie horde.

to prior silver-screen zombies, Romero's walking dead followed no evil master, and for the first time possessed an insatiable appetite for living flesh. Yet despite his divergence from traditional zombie lore, and not one reference or mention of the word "zombie" in the film, cinemagoers nevertheless identified them as such, and the moniker stuck. "[Finally] I said, maybe they are zombies," Romero recalls affably. "So I called them zombies in [the sequel] *Dawn of the Dead* [1978]. I finally used the word, 'zombie'!" This cemented a further deviation from the zombie's Haitian and voodoo origins. As *Night of the Living Dead* unfolds, the audience and the besieged on-screen victims discover together the mysteries and rules for this new modern breed of walking dead.

When Barbara finally reaches the deserted, white two-story farmhouse, she rushes inside and locks the door. So she grabs a butcher knife for protection and has a look around the shadowy dwelling—an actual farmhouse, it became the film's central shooting location. With the production's limited resources, there was no money to build the house as a set. Fortunately, the filmmakers heard about an abandoned farmhouse that was scheduled to be demolished in Evans City, about forty miles north of Pittsburgh. The owners rented it to the production for three hundred dollars a month, and although it had no running water, the production team was able to dress the house to look lived in, and then slowly tear it apart as the script required.

Just as Barbara bolts out the farmhouse door in a panic, a black man (Duane Jones), also seeking refuge, pulls up in a pickup truck. He immediately jumps into action and fights off three zombies, killing them by bashing their heads in with a tire iron. He later drags one of the zombie corpses outside and lights it on fire, frightening off the growing number of ghouls amassing around the house—they're hypersensitive to fire. Then the hammering starts. He begins barricading the windows and doors with any piece of board or stick of furniture he can find, all

Overleaf: Italian theatrical poster for
Night of the Living Dead (page 80);
British poster (page 81, top); military one-
sheet (page 81, bottom left); Australian
one-sheet (page 81, bottom right).

FEAR

that deadliest of all emotions clutching at your heart the....

NIGHT OF THE LIVING DEAD. X

starring JUDITH O'DEA · DUANE JONES · MARILYN EASTMAN · KARL HARDMAN · JUDITH RIDLEY · KEITH WAYNE

Produced by Russell W. Streiner and Karl Hardman · Directed by George A. Romero · Sceenplay by John A. Russo · A Walter Reade Organisation Presentation   Distribututon by Monarch Film Corporation Ltd.

**They Rise to Devour the Living!
More Terrifying than Hitchcock's
"PSYCHO"!**

NIGHT OF THE LIVING DEAD

JUDITH O'DEA
RUSSELL STREINER
DUANE JONES

a CONTINENTAL Picture

SOMETHING NEW   SOMETHING EVIL
SOMETHING UNSPEAKABLY TERRIFYING

NIGHT OF THE LIVING DEAD Ⓜ

NO LOVE STORY, NO HERO,
NO HEROINE, NO MESSAGE,
NO QUESTIONS, NO ANSWERS

JUST TERROR
WHICH GNAWS AT YOUR VERY
BEING

Starring JUDITH O'DEA · DUANE JONES · MARILYN EASTMAN · KARL HARDMAN · JUDITH RIDLEY · KEITH WAYNE
Produced by Russell W. Streiner and Karl Hardman · Directed by George A. Romero · Screenplay by John A. Russo

the while explaining to Barbara, as best as he can, what he's been able to piece together from what he's witnessed. While it's finally reassuring to have a heroic character take the lead and make the audience feel safe, *Night of the Living Dead* was released during the height of the civil rights movement in America, six months after Martin Luther King, Jr., was assassinated. Parts of the country were still racially divided and unwilling to accept a black man as a heroic lead in a motion picture. Some exhibitors refused to even screen the film. Not only was Jones's portrayal of Ben a stark contrast to those played by Willie Best and Mantan Moreland in *Ghost Breakers* (1940) and *King of the Zombies* (1941), but the character's race wasn't even addressed in the film as well. However, due to the volatile times in which it was released, there was a lot of conjecture about its racial themes. "Now all of the sudden it was a 'black film.' It became a 'black film,' even though when Jack Russo and I wrote the script, the character in the script, we assumed him to be white," recalled Romero. But after selecting Jones for the role, the filmmakers felt no reason to alter the script. "We cast a black man not because he was black, but because we liked Duane's audition better than the others we had seen. Perhaps *Night of the Living Dead* is the first film to have a black man playing the lead role regardless of, rather than because of, his color, and in that sense the observation of the fact is valid, but we did not calculate that this would be an attention-grabber. We backed into it," admitted the writer-director. "Our own relaxed, honest, uninhibited naïve attitudes as we approached the production ultimately read out as unconscious elements in the picture, which added to its realism, offhandedness, and uniqueness."

As the movie progresses and night deepens, Ben and Barbara discover that they are not alone in the farmhouse. Emerging from the cellar are a teen couple and a husband and wife with an injured daughter. They've been hiding there for hours, believing it's the safest place. When the group finds a TV set, they huddle

around for a series of live, up-to-the-minute television updates of the national crisis, eerily reminiscent of Walter Cronkite's tense live news reports about President John F. Kennedy's assassination in Dallas. This staging added tension and credibility to the story's fantastical premise. ". . . I think we have some late word just arriving. Let me interrupt to bring this to you," the reporter announces with urgency from a noisy newsroom, as a colleague passes him a document. "This is the latest disclosure in a report from National Civil Defense Headquarters in Washington: It has been established that persons who have recently died have been returning to life, and committing acts of murder. A widespread investigation of reports from funeral homes, morgues, and hospitals has concluded that the unburied dead are coming back to life and seeking human victims. It's hard for us here to believe what we're reporting to you, but it does seem to be a fact." Then when the reporter advises citizens to get to a local rescue station, a disagreement erupts in the living room. While the group quarrels over who should be in charge and what they should do next, the flesh eaters continue to amass outside.

The film gives no concrete cause behind these inexplicable events, other than rumored news reports tying the "mutations" to mysterious levels of radiation from a NASA Venus probe. "I thought it was some sort of punishment, something was happening that was beyond our understanding," explains Romero. "I felt that it didn't matter at all. What should matter is that this extraordinary thing is happening and people are still arguing about upstairs, downstairs, who's the boss? They're still arguing about their own agendas, instead of facing the problem. And that's really what all of my zombie films have been about." Romero also directed for naturalism, eschewing the sanitized camp seen in previous zombie films. He implemented violence and gore for a purpose, and unraveled the course of events realistically on an interpersonal level, culminating in a bleak and pessimistic outcome that delivers his sobering message about the disintegration of society—about the living, not the dead.

Above: Harry (Karl Hardman) and Helen (Marilyn Eastman) hunker down in the farmhouse cellar with their ailing daughter Karen (Kyra Schon).

Opposite: Barbara (Judith O'Dea), Ben (Duane Jones), and Tom (Keith Wayne) grapple with inexplicable events. Unlike any films at the time, *Night of the Living Dead* hit a cultural nerve by featuring a black lead and no mention of race.

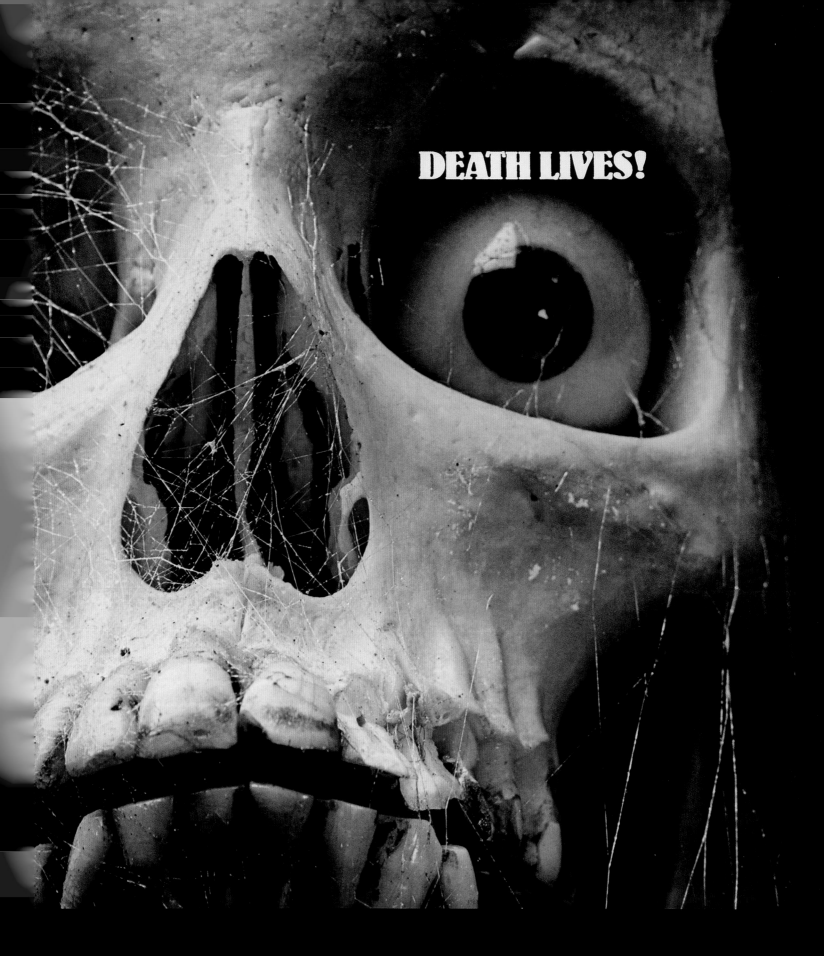

DEATH LIVES!

"TALES FROM THE CRYPT"

5 THE INFECTION SPREADS

Opposite: Theatrical poster for *Tales from the Crypt* (1972).

The enormous success and controversial reception of *Night of the Living Dead* (1968) reinvigorated the genre, not only sparking a global outbreak of zombie-laced films in the 1970s, but also launching a protracted horror boom not seen since the 1930s. While the major Hollywood studios remained reluctant to embrace the living dead, a wide array of independent producers in the United States and around the world began churning out an eclectic and sometimes peculiar assortment of low-budget exploitation films featuring zombies, their attempt at enticing the youth market with enhanced gore, occasional nudity, shamelessly derivative concepts, and socially progressive themes.

One of the most popular horror films from the early 1970s was the first feature-film adaptation of the hugely influential and popular horror comic of the 1950s, EC Comic's *Tales from the Crypt* (1972). George A. Romero even credited the original pulpy comic book series for their nostalgic influence on *Night of the Living Dead*. Directed by Freddie Francis, this British anthology film, courtesy of Amicus Productions, features multiple Academy Award– and Tony Award–nominee and BAFTA winner Ralph Richardson as the infamous crypt keeper who presides as host over the five terrifying tales. The most noteworthy segment was *Poetic Justice*, which stars horror veteran Peter Cushing, known outside the genre for playing Grand Moff Tarkin in *Star Wars* (1977). In this third tale of the series, Cushing is Arthur Edward Grimsdyke, a misunderstood widower who is driven to suicide by his heartless neighbors but who rises from the grave as a decaying zombie to deliver a vengeful, ghastly lesson.

Children Shouldn't Play with Dead Things (1972), shot over fourteen days in Miami for $70,000, is a satirical take on *Night of the Living Dead* geared squarely at the youth market, and written by Alan Ormsby and Bob Clark, with Ormsby starring in and Clark directing the film. Clark's more iconic films include *Porky's* (1982) and *A Christmas Story* (1983). The story follows a theater troupe led by practical joker Alan (Ormsby). Looking to have some fun for the night, they take a short trip to a small island where criminals are buried. Alan fools the group into believing that he's raised the dead through his séances. It's all in good fun, until the grisly-looking, flesh-eating dead actually begin rising from their graves looking for payback.

On the peculiar side is *Psychomania* (a.k.a. *Death Wheelers* [1972]), a British film riding on the coattails of two then-recent but disparate hits: Dennis Hopper's motorcycle opus *Easy Rider* (1969) and *Night of the Living Dead*'s trending zombies. This amalgam of motifs centers on young rebel Tom Latham (Nicky Henson), who convinces his skull-helmeted biker gang, "The Living Dead," that he's found a way to cheat death through suicide. Most of the gang follow him back from the

Above: Arthur Grimsdyke (Peter Cushing) returns from the grave to settle a score in *Tales from the Crypt*.

Opposite: Theatrical poster for Alan Ormsby and Benjamin "Bob" Clark's *Children Shouldn't Play with Dead Things* (1972).

Pages 88-89: Theatrical posters for *Psychomania* (a.k.a *Death Wheelers* [1972]) and *The House of Seven Corpses* (1974).

grave—he's buried sitting upright on his bike—returning as unstoppable zombie bikers, intent on terrorizing English locals forever.

A distinctly unconventional zombie picture, *Messiah of Evil* (1973), from husband-and-wife team Willard Huyck and Gloria Katz, is mostly inspired by European art-house films. After completing a film treatment for George Lucas's coming-of-age hit *American Graffiti* (1973), the two recent University of Southern California film school alums heard that their former agent had come into some financing. He approached them with a chance to make their own movie, but the stipulation was that it needed to be a horror picture. The couple, also known for scripting *Indiana Jones and the Temple of Doom* (1984), which contains a nostalgic throwback to Monogram's zombie pictures, came up with the premise for *Messiah of Evil* in a few weeks.

Prompted by a series of letters from her father (Royal Dano), Arletty (Marianna Hill) travels to the California seaside town of Point Dune, where she discovers a town populated by evil. Moving in droves and bleeding from their eyes, these local ghouls also consume living flesh. But the dreamlike quality of the film makes it unlike previous entries. "What influenced us, having just finished film school not long before, was sort of art films," recalled Huyck. "You know, Italian films, Antonioni, Goddard, things like that. So the film has a strange sort of pretentious art-film quality, at the same time as trying to be a horror film." Katz added, "And then the French were very, very heavy into voice-over and into literary allusions, so that's what we were interested in. It had nothing to do with what the investors wanted to do."

THE DEAD STILL RIDE...

the Living Howl in TERROR!

THE DEATH WHEELERS

starring

GEORGE SANDERS
BERYL REID
NICKY HENSON
MARY LARKIN

with ROY HOLDER , ROBERT HARDY , PATRICK HOLT , DENIS GILMORE

produced by ANDREW DONALLY, directed by DON SHARP, written by ARNAUD D'USSEAU

color by TECHNICOLOR A SCOTIA INTERNATIONAL RELEASE PG PARENTAL GUIDANCE SUGGESTED
Some material may not be suitable for pre-teenagers

73/235

"THE DEATH WHEELERS"

EIGHT GRAVES!
SEVEN BODIES!
ONE KILLER...AND HE'S ALREADY DEAD.

THE HOUSE OF SEVEN CORPSES

AN INTERNATIONAL AMUSEMENTS CORPORATION RELEASE OF A TCA PRODUCTION
Starring JOHN IRELAND / FAITH DOMERGUE / JOHN CARRADINE / CAROLE WELLS
Written, Produced & Directed by PAUL HARRISON / COLOR

PG PARENTAL GUIDANCE SUGGESTED
SOME MATERIAL MAY NOT BE
SUITABLE FOR PRE-TEENAGERS

74/ 20

Above: Diana "Sugar" Hill (Marki Bey) and her zombie henchmen in *Sugar Hill* (1974).

Opposite: Movie poster announcing funk, soul, and zombies in director Paul Maslansky's blaxploitation film *Sugar Hill*.

Filmmaker Paul Harrison took a more populist approach with his movie-within-a-movie, *The House of Seven Corpses* (1974), which refers to a cursed Victorian mansion, once home to the Beal family, who meddled with the occult and suffered violent deaths. When a narcissistic film director (John Ireland) and his cast and crew move in to shoot their new horror movie, they ignore warnings by the resident caretaker (John Carradine), and incorporate passages into the film from a mysterious book entitled "The Tibetan Book of the Dead." Soon, a rotting zombie rises from the family cemetery and begins killing the film's crew.

Along with the revival of the supernatural component, another group of films revisited the traditional implementation of zombies as henchmen, cropping up in films like *Sugar Hill* (1974), *Shanks* (1974), *The Child* (1977), and *Shock Waves* (1977). Even traditional voodoo elements resurfaced in the blaxploitation romp *Sugar Hill*. Targeted to the urban black market, blaxploitation films of the mid-1970s featured a primarily black cast and soundtracks replete with funk and soul. But *Sugar Hill* offers a bonus—zombies! Diana "Sugar" Hill (Marki Bey) refuses to be intimidated by a gang of thugs who murdered her fiancé. Sugar turns to high voodoo priestess Mama Maitresse (Zara Cully, Mother Jefferson from TV's *The Jeffersons*) and witchdoctor Baron Samedi (Don Pedro Colley) to summon a legion of native zombies with bulging silver-pinball eyes, reminiscent of Carrefour from *I Walked with a Zombie* (1943). In her tailored white jumpsuit and perfectly coifed afro, Sugar confronts one of the thugs: "Hey whitey, you and your punk friends killed my man!" Then, just before unleashing her machete-wielding zombies

Meet SUGAR HILL and her ZOMBIE HIT MEN...

—The Mafia has never met anything like them!

Sugar Hill

SAMUEL Z. ARKOFF Presents   Color by Movielab **PG** PARENTAL GUIDANCE SUGGESTED

"SUGAR HILL" Starring MARKI BEY · ROBERT QUARRY · DON PEDRO COLLEY

Co-Starring BETTY ANNE REES · RICHARD LAWSON · ZARA CULLY · Written by TIM KELLY · Produced by ELLIOTT SCHICK
Directed by PAUL MASLANSKY Original Music Composed by NICK ZESSES and DINO FEKARIS · an American International Picture

74/59

"SUGAR HILL"

to even the score, she asserts, "I'm not accusing you, honk. I'm passing sentence. . . . And the sentence is death!"

One of the more offbeat zombie films of the era, *Shanks*, paired legendary schlock director and showman William Castle (*House on Haunted Hill* [1959], *The Tingler* [1959]) with the internationally renowned mime Marcel Marceau, at Paramount Pictures. Castle, a moviemaker noted for his previous B-movie chillers and promotional gimmicks, had just produced the enormously successful A-film *Rosemary's Baby* (1968) for the studio. Marceau, recognized for his comic-tragic clown Bip, traded in his striped jersey, whiteface makeup, and battered stovepipe hat to portray two very different characters in this most unusual horror film. "It was exactly what I had been looking for," professed Marceau, who had been searching for the ideal cinematic vehicle. Marceau plays deaf-mute puppeteer Malcolm Shanks, as well as Old Walker, a white-haired scientist who takes Shanks under his wing as a lab assistant. When Walker dies, Shanks uses the scientist's experiments to reanimate the dead and manipulate them like marionettes to exact his revenge on those who have been cruel to him. Rather than reanimating corpses through science experiments, director Robert Voskanian's *The Child* (1977) seems to imply that telekinesis is responsible for making the dead walk, in this ultra-low-budget *Carrie* (1976) derivative. The film proves that telekinetic powers in the hands of a twisted child who lives near a cemetery can generate zombies—and she unleashes her ghastly ghouls to exact punishment on everyone she dislikes.

While some of these movies restored the zombie archetype to its more traditional rank of henchman, *Shock Waves* (1977) echoes John Carradine's

Above: Sugar (Marki Bey) and voodoo priestess Mama Maitresse (Zara Cully) summon the zombies in *Sugar Hill*.

Opposite: Machete-wielding zombie hit men unchained in *Sugar Hill*.

Left, Above, and Opposite

Above: Renowned mime Marcel Marceau puppeteers the dead in director William Castle's eccentric offering *Shanks* (1974).

Opposite Below: Film posters for *Shanks* (left) and the ultra-low-budget *The Child* (1977) (right).

DELICIOUSLY GROTESQUE

A new concept in the macabre in which
the Good come out of the grave
and the Evil are sent to fill the vacancy.

Paramount Pictures presents
a william castle production
marcel marceau in
shanks
co-starring
philippe clay tsilla chelton
music scored by alex north
written by ranald graham produced by steven north directed by william castle in color
a paramount picture

LET'S PLAY HIDE AND GO KILL....!

THE
CHILD

A
HARRY
NOVAK
presentation

color by EASTMANCOLOR

mad-scientist aspirations from *Revenge of the Zombies* (1943). Vestiges of a secret Nazi super-soldier experiment resurface in modern times when a small commercial yacht is struck by a mysterious ship in dark open waters. In an ironic twist, Carradine plays the salty yacht captain who turns up dead the next morning. The boaters take refuge in a nearby remote tropical island, where they meet the sole inhabitant of a rundown hotel (shot at the then-rundown Biltmore Hotel in Coral Gables, Florida), where a reclusive old man (Peter Cushing) with a German accent has a heck of a tale. "We Germans developed the perfect weapon—a soldier," he says earnestly. "They were the most vicious and bloodthirsty of all the SS divisions. The group under my command was designed for the water, to man submarines we should never have to service. . . . We created the perfect soldier from cheap hoodlums and thugs, and a good number of pathological murderers and sadists as well. We called them *Der Toten Korps*— 'The Death Corps.' Creatures more horrible than any you can imagine. Not dead, not alive, but somewhere in between." After the Germans lost the war, Cushing's character sunk the ship with the Death Corps on board, and then migrated to the secluded island. "And now she has returned," he says soberly. Walking the ocean floor, reminiscent of the aquatic dead from *Zombies of Mora Tau* (1957), these mute Nazi zombies have pasty complexions, withered and pruned, and are fully clad in their SS-issued uniforms and black sun goggles—without which they founder. Seemingly inspired by *Jaws* (1975), the hit movie of the era, every zombie attack has an aquatic motif, generally preceded by a shot of a zombie under the surface, followed by it slowly rising up from the depths for the ambush.

Also integrating past historical events with the subgenre's zombie lore was a quartet of films from Spain known as the *Blind Dead* series, written and directed by Amando de Ossorio. These walking dead are preceded by a medieval back story, which Osorrio fashioned after the Order of the Knights Templar from the Middle Ages, but who returned from the Crusades worshipping black magic. Upon their return, they ravaged the countryside and sacrificed every virgin girl in the village as part of their death rituals. When the king conquered them, they were excommunicated and hanged for their heresy. The crows ate the eyes out of the cadavers as they rotted on the gallows, leaving them blind. Echoing synonymously with their presence on-screen are the sounds of demonic Gregorian chants, heard as the "Blind Dead" rise from their crypts to terrorize the twentieth century: decayed skeletal corpses with no eyes, outfitted with swords and hooded cloaks, resembling grim reapers and pursuing victims on their zombie horses. While these knights have no eyes to see, they can hear the slightest sound, even tracking their prey through the pounding of their terrified hearts.

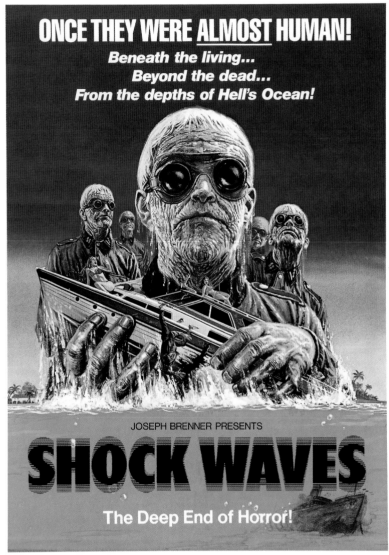

Above: Nazi zombies surge into theaters on the film poster for *Shock Waves* (1977).

Opposite: Peter Cushing is a reclusive German SS Commander forced to confront his past indiscretions in *Shock Waves*.

LIVING DEAD MEN—
Existing on the FLESH of
the YOUNG & BEAUTIFUL!

HORROR
OF THE
ZOMBIES

starring MARIA PERSCHY • JACK TAYLOR
in EASTMAN COLOR   an INDEPENDENT-INTERNATIONAL release
R RESTRICTED

Below: Spanish film posters for *Tombs of the Blind Dead* (*La noche del terror ciego* [1972]) and *The Ghost Galleon* (*El buque maldito*).

LA NOCHE DEL TERROR CIEGO

CESAR   LONE   HELEN   JOSEPH
BURNER · FLEMING · HARP · THELMAN

DIRECTOR
AMANDO
DE OSSORIO   TECHNICOLOR   70m/m   UNA COPRODUCCION
PLATA FILMS (MADRID)
INTERFILME P.C. (LISBOA)

MARIA PERSCHY   JACK TAYLOR
CARLOS LEMOS   BARBARA REY
MANUEL DE BLAS   BLANCA ESTRADA

EASTMANCOLOR

EL BUQUE MALDITO

director: AMANDO DE OSSORIO   EN PRODUCCION ANCLA CENTURY FILMS PARA BELEN FILMS

Opposite: Medieval knights rise from their crypts to terrorize present-day Spain in director Amando de Ossorio's *Blind Dead* movie series.

Above: American film poster for *The Ghost Galleon* (*El buque maldito* [1974]) labels it *Horror of the Zombies.*

Right: Spanish film poster for *Return of the Blind Dead* (*El ataque de los muertos sin ojos* [1973]).

TONY KENDALL
FERNANDO SANCHO ESPERANZA ROY
EL ATAQUE DE LOS
MUERTOS SIN OJOS

STOP....HALTE AUX PESTICIDES....STOP....VILLAGES
ET VIGNES CONTAMINES..STOP..URGENT SECOURS

Claude GUEDJ
présente :

LES
RAISINS
DE LA
MORT !

un film de Jean ROLLIN

Above: Tainted wine produces local zombies in the French *The Grapes of Death* (*Les raisins de la mort* [1978]).

Top Right: Skeletal corpses from the past threaten the present in the *Blind Dead* movie series from Spain.

Opposite: Film poster touts a tale of vengeful zombie inmates in *Garden of the Dead* (1972).

Although their first victim returns from the dead as a bloodthirsty zombie in the first installment of the series, *Tombs of the Blind Dead* (*La noche del terror ciego* [1972]), this concept was an anomaly. Subsequent films, *Return of the Blind Dead* (*El ataque de los muertos sin ojos* [1973]), *The Ghost Galleon* (*El buque maldito* [1974]), and *Night of the Seagulls* (*La noche de las gaviotas* [1975]), continued to develop the legacy of the Blind Dead as a decaying, unyielding representation of the past that rises up to destroy modern society, solidifying the series' grim vision of death's certainty.

Toxic contaminants are also capable of spreading zombie outbreaks, as seen in *Garden of the Dead* (1972), *Let Sleeping Corpses Lie* (a.k.a. *The Living Dead at Manchester Morgue* [1974]), and *The Grapes of Death* (*Les raisins de la mort* [1978]). Working with a shoestring budget, director John Hayes brought back a group of dead prison inmates in the double-bill cofeature *Garden of the Dead*. When convicts at a remote prison work camp become addicted to some experimental formaldehyde produced there, they grow unruly and are shot and killed during a planned prison break. After being buried in unmarked graves nearby, their corpses return to the prison as vengeful, occasionally vocal, zombies.

In the French shocker *The Grapes of Death* (*Les raisins de la mort*), bad pesticide is responsible for contaminating the wine and turning the French countryside locals into meanspirited "living" (yet gradually decomposing) zombies. Director Jean Rollin and producer Claude Guedj patterned the structure of their zombie adventure after popular 1970s disaster films such as *The Poseidon Adventure* (1972), where characters are continually moving from place to place in order to survive. In effect, they created a mobile variation of *Night of the Living Dead*, which conversely traps the characters in one location.

Most closely paralleling the nihilistic tone and structure of Romero's *Living Dead* is Spanish director Jorge Grau's Italian/Spanish coproduction *Let Sleeping Corpses Lie* (a.k.a. *The Living Dead at Manchester Morgue*), practically a European reinterpretation of *Night of the Living Dead*. Culpability for this zombie apocalypse is traced to the Ministry of Agriculture, which unintentionally reanimates the dead via an experimental radiation-emitting device, intended as an innocuous pesticide. Caught in the English countryside amid the zombie uprising are George (Ray Lovelock) and Edna (Cristina Galbo). Brought together by fate, the pair must ward off not only the zombies, but also an impulsive old police sergeant played by Arthur Kennedy, who suspects them and their young "hippie" kind of carrying out the cannibalistic murders. The film's exteriors were shot on location in England, and the use of color photography and ghastly makeup amplified the gore to disturbing new heights for the period.

"GARDEN OF THE DEAD"

臓物をひっぱり出して喰いたい！重い墓石をはねのけて、冷たい土の中から一斉に立上った死人たち！かさぶたをはがして生血を吸いたい！

悪魔シリーズ第3弾

いけにえ

悪魔の墓場

LET SLEEPING
CORPSES LIE

〈カラー作品〉

Das Leichenhaus der Lebenden Toten

(THE LIVING DEAD AT THE MANCHESTER MORGUE)

ARTHUR KENNEDY, Ray Lovelock, Christine Galbo, William Lyton
Regie: George Grau   Produktion: Flamina Cinematografiche S.R.L./ Profilm

RAY LOVELOCK   CHRISTINE GALBO

ARTHUR KENNEDY

NON SI DEVE PROFANARE IL SONNO DEI MORTI

ALDO MASSASSO • VERA DRUDY • GIORGIO TRESTINI • GENGHER GATTI

CROMOCOLOR   REGIA DI JORGE GRAU
EASTMANCOLOR

THEY TAMPERED WITH NATURE –
NOW THEY MUST PAY THE PRICE...

TO AVOID
FAINTING
KEEP REPEATING,
IT'S ONLY A MOVIE
..ONLY A MOVIE
..ONLY A MOVIE
.ONLY A MOVIE
.ONLY A MOVIE
ONLY A MOVIE

R

"DON'T OPEN
THE WINDOW"

WHAT EVER'S OUT THERE WILL WAIT !

◆ A Newport Release ◆

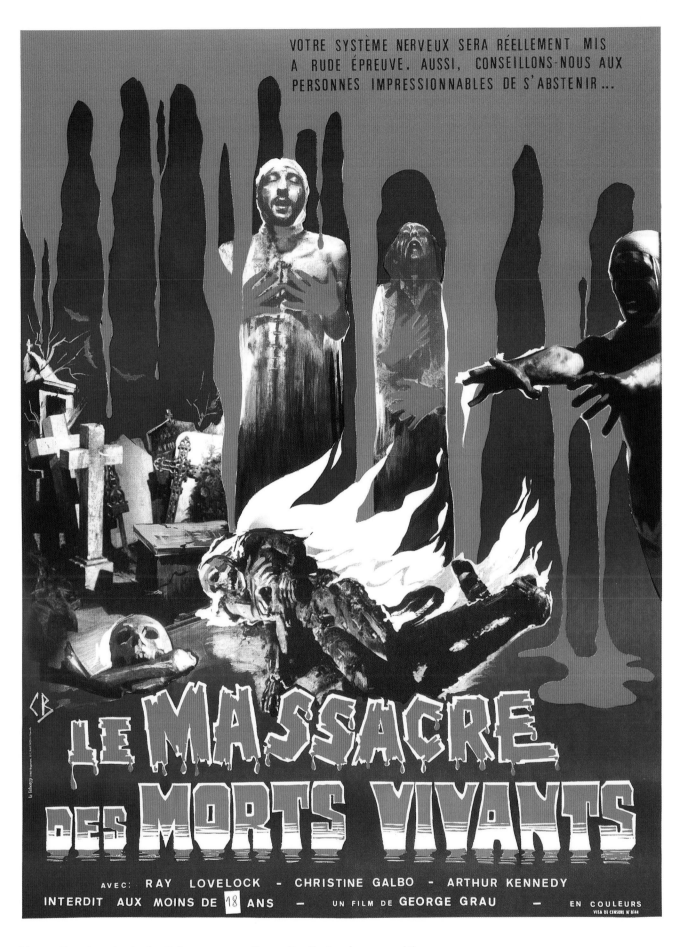

VOTRE SYSTÈME NERVEUX SERA RÉELLEMENT MIS À RUDE ÉPREUVE. AUSSI, CONSEILLONS-NOUS AUX PERSONNES IMPRESSIONNABLES DE S'ABSTENIR...

LE MASSACRE DES MORTS VIVANTS

AVEC: RAY LOVELOCK - CHRISTINE GALBO - ARTHUR KENNEDY

INTERDIT AUX MOINS DE 18 ANS - UN FILM DE GEORGE GRAU - EN COULEURS

VISA DE CENSURE N° 0744

Above: French poster for the Italian-Spanish coproduction *Let Sleeping Corpses Lie* (a.k.a. *The Living Dead at Manchester Morgue* [1974]).

Opposite: Posters from around the world for director Jorge Grau's *Let Sleeping Corpses Lie* (a.k.a. *The Living Dead at Manchester Morgue*).

When there's no more room in HELL the dead will walk the EARTH

First there was
'**NIGHT** OF THE **LIVING DEAD**'

Now
GEORGE A. ROMERO'S

DAWN OF THE DEAD

HERBERT R. STEINMANN & BILLY BAXTER PRESENT A LAUREL GROUP PRODUCTION in Association with CLAUDIO ARGENTO & ALFREDO CUOMO

Starring: **DAVID EMGE** **KEN FOREE** **SCOTT H. REINIGER** **GAYLEN ROSS**

Director of Photography: MICHAEL GORNICK   Music By: THE GOBLINS with DARIO ARGENTO

Produced By: **RICHARD P. RUBINSTEIN** Written and Directed by: **GEORGE A. ROMERO**

READ THE ST. MARTIN'S BOOK   TECHNICOLOR®   ©DAWN ASSOCIATES MCMLXXVIII   Released by UNITED FILM DISTRIBUTION CO.

> There is no explicit sex in this picture.
> However, there are scenes of violence which may be considered shocking.
> No one under 17 will be admitted.

As the 1970s came to a close, cinemagoers caught a movie trailer announcing what became one of the most anticipated zombie movies of all time. A title crawl, accompanied by an ominous voice-over, came over a graphic of what appeared to be a sun rising over a distant horizon: "In 1968 George Romero brought us 'Night of the Living Dead.' It became the classic horror film of its time. Now, George Romero brings us the most intensely shocking motion picture experience for all times. Dawn of the Dead. Night of the Living Dead has ended. Dawn of the Dead is here." Cue the cheering fans. A decade after Romero made the watershed *Night of the Living Dead*, he was back with the follow-up, *Dawn of the Dead* (1978). For years, Romero resisted doing another *Living Dead* film, uncertain he'd be able to duplicate the fortuitous circumstances that had made the first film a classic. But an invitation to a shopping mall changed all that, recalled Romero. "It was the first indoor shopping mall that we had ever seen, that anyone had ever seen in Western Pennsylvania. I went out a few days before it opened and I saw all these trucks coming in with everything that Americans could ever want, and I said, 'Wow, this is like a temple to consumerism.' And that's where the thought came from. Then I started to write a script that had that at its core." Unable to secure any independent financing domestically, Romero and producer Richard Rubinstein found the support they needed to make *Dawn of the Dead* from Italian horror filmmaker Dario Argento, who helped secure its reported $650,000 production cost. Argento also invited Romero to Rome to continue writing. The events in the film pick up directly after *Night of the Living Dead*, as the zombie phenomenon

This Spread: Film still and poster for Romero's highly-anticipated follow-up, *Dawn of the Dead* (1978).

continues to spread. Martial law has become ineffective at maintaining the social order in a disintegrating society that still can't set aside differences in order to find common solutions. Two Philadelphia SWAT officers, Peter (Ken Foree) and Roger (Scott H. Reiniger), a pregnant news station producer, Fran (Gaylen Ross), and her boyfriend Stephen (David Emge), escape the city in a stolen news helicopter and find refuge in a sprawling suburban shopping mall, where they have everything they could ever want to start a new life—if they can fend off the zombie horde and a gang of looters.

Romero infused *Dawn of the Dead* with satirical jabs at excess consumerism, correlating the roaming zombies to shallow mall shoppers. These zombies exhibit a form of sense memory, as the character Peter explains: "They don't know why they're here. They just remember, remember that they want to be in here." *Dawn*'s living dead aren't just faceless masses either; each corpse has its own unique personality that individuates its gray pallor. The Hare Krishna zombie is most memorable. "I wanted them to have a past, and so there's a nun, a softball player. . . . Even just with wardrobe, I tried to make them familiar," asserted Romero. "What the hell are they?" asks Fran. "They're us," remarks Peter. "You know Macumba? Voodoo. Granddad was a priest in Trinidad. He used to tell us, 'When there's no more room in Hell, the dead will walk the Earth.'"

Although *Dawn of the Dead* is a sequel, Romero took risks, and gave it a style and tone all its own. The biting satire was shot in vivid color, and in mostly brightly lit interiors at the actual Monroeville shopping mall that initially inspired him. While the hue of the blood was intentionally pushed to give it a bright-red comic-book appearance, the unsettling graphic nature of Tom Savini's special makeup effects earned the film the commercially toxic X rating from the Motion Picture Association of America. Romero and his producers rejected the rating and released the film unrated, adding in its place, this disclaimer: "There is no explicit sex in this picture, however there are scenes of violence which may be considered shocking. No one under 17 will be admitted." *Dawn of the Dead* went on to gross $55 million worldwide, and its success wasn't limited to ticket sales. Respected film critic Roger Ebert hailed the independent film as "one of the best horror films ever made." With *Dawn of the Dead*, Romero had permanently cemented his apocalyptic vision of flesh-eating zombies onto the subgenre, and there was no turning back.

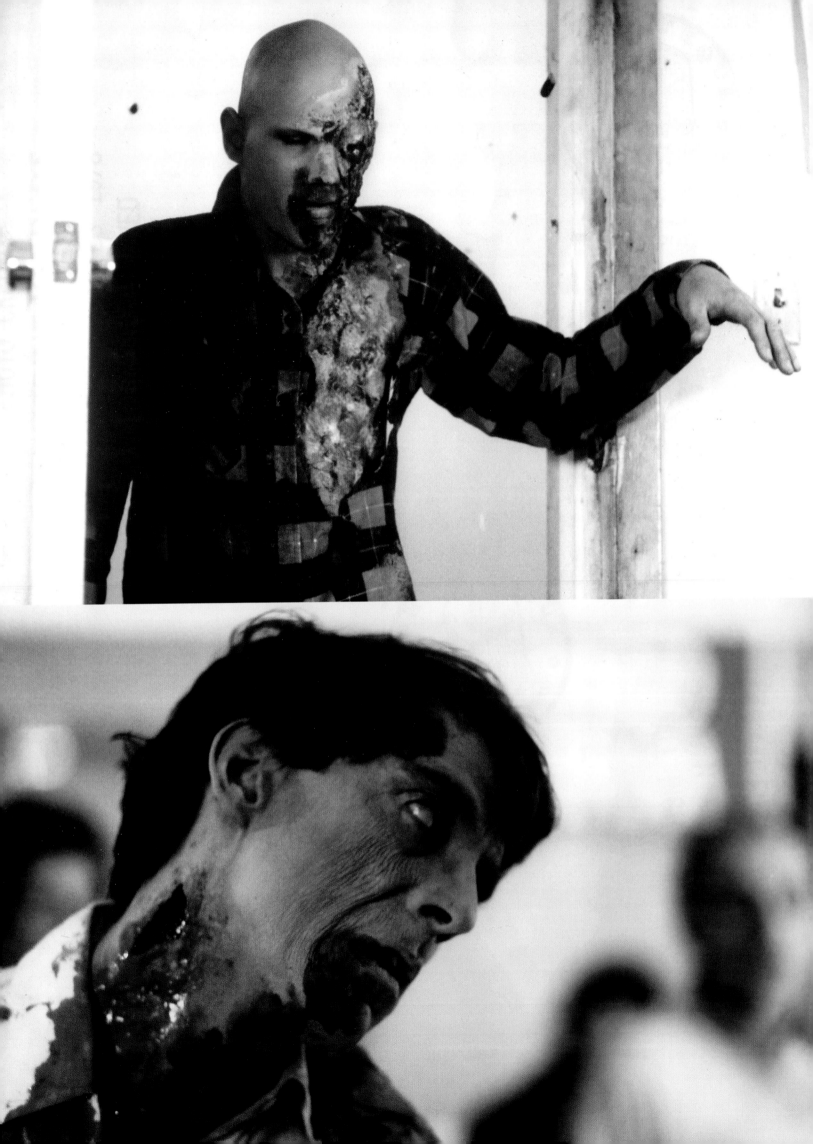

WE ARE GOING TO EAT YOU!

ZOMBIE

...THE DEAD ARE AMONG US!

Jerry Gross presents "ZOMBIE" starring Tisa Farrow • Ian McCulloch • Richard Johnson • Al Cliver
Story and Screenplay by Elisa Briganti • Produced by Ugo Tucci and Fabrizio De Angelis for Variety Film
Color by Metro Color • Directed by Lucio Fulci • Distributed by The Jerry Gross Organization

6 SPLATTER RUNS THICK

y the 1980s, the burgeoning home video and cable television markets offered film producers additional exhibition outlets for their low-budget zombie content. Like drive-ins beforehand, these two new peripheral mediums were extremely popular with young audiences and contributed to a historic rise of zombie film production worldwide. To remain competitive, filmmakers employed the latest advances in special makeup effects, designing bold new gags that promised gross-out spectacle like never before. Romero described the over-the-top, gory effects in *Dawn of the Dead* (1978) as "splatter cinema." The term stuck, and so did the trend—especially in Italy, with filmmaker Lucio Fulci.

Fulci's Italian-made cult classic *Zombie* (*Zombi 2* [1979]), marked the director's first foray into the living dead subgenre, and it is still hailed by fans as one of the best. The film was released in the United States in 1980, but without the "2" in the title. In order to capitalize on the success of *Dawn of the Dead*, which had been released in Europe as *Zombi,* the August 1979 Italian release brazenly bore the title *Zombi 2*. While the unauthorized follow-up borrows heavily from Romero's zombie mythos, it embraces escapism over social commentary. The film's big stars are Giannetto De Rossi's practical makeup effects, a gruesome leap forward from his previous work on *Let Sleeping Corpses Lie* (a.k.a. *The Living Dead at Manchester Morgue* [1974]). Fulci and De Rossi's splatter extravaganza depicts decayed maggot-filled corpses, torn flesh, dismembered bodies, and an iconic squirm-inducing sequence where a splintered wooden spike slowly impales a woman through her eyeball!

Working off a script by Elisa Briganti and Dardano Sacchetti, Fulci found inspiration not only from Romero; he also credited the classic *I Walked with a Zombie* (1943) as a key source. In *Zombie*, he reintroduces the zombie's traditional Caribbean voodoo origins and links them to Romero's urban flesh eaters. Starring a mix of American and European actors, the poor dubbing is offset by the film's glorious widescreen photography. The story unfolds with a mystery, and an abandoned sailboat drifting aimlessly in New York harbor. But when boarded by two coast guard officers, a zombie lunges out from below deck and attacks one of them. His partner unloads his gun on the zombie until its bullet-riddled body falls overboard into the drink. Searching for answers are Peter (Ian McCulloch), an intrepid reporter, and Anne, the missing boat owner's vulnerable daughter, played by Tisa Farrow—a spitting image of sister Mia (*Rosemary's Baby* [1968], *The Great Gatsby* [1974]). The two join up and set off to find her father in the Caribbean. They discover the tiny island of Matul with the help of a young couple, whose boat they charter—but not before an unforgettable sequence involving an underwater

Opposite: Poster for director Lucio Fulci's cult classic *Zombie* (*Zombi 2* [1979]).

Below: A struggle between Paola (Olga Karlatos) and a zombie attacker in *Zombie* (*Zombi 2*) leads to one of the most shockingly "eye-conic" moments in undead cinema.

Overleaf: Fulci ushered in a new age of visceral gore to the horror subgenre.

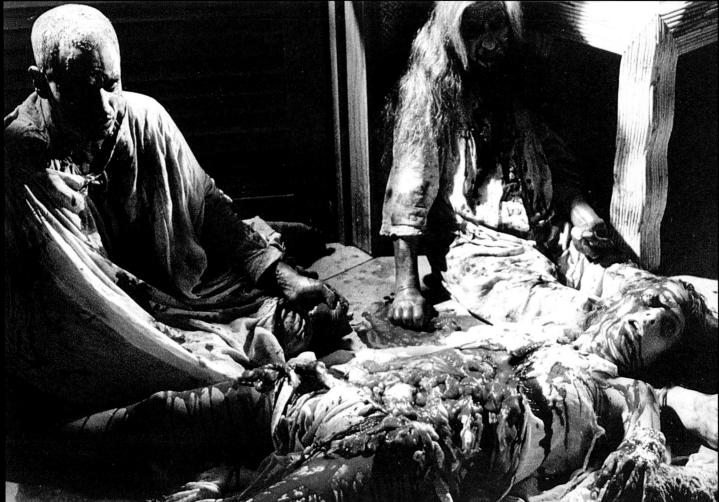

Above: A ravenous stowaway arrives in New York harbor in *Zombie* (*Zombi 2*).

Opposite: French film poster for *Oasis of the Zombies* (*L'abime des morts vivants; La tumba de los muertos vivientes* [1982]).

zombie versus a live shark! On Matul, they join Dr. Menard's (Richard Johnson) gory struggle in an effort to contain an unstoppable zombie epidemic, culminating in a fiery show-stopping climax.

Emboldened by the global financial success of Fulci's *Zombie*, Italian and Spanish producers unleashed a pandemic of low-budget European zombie derivatives, sequels, and imitators into the marketplace. None were able to duplicate their progenitor's achievements, but they nevertheless vied to cash in on the trend, with films like *Nightmare City* (*Incubosulla citta contaminata* [1980]), *Cannibal Apocalypse* (*Apocalypse domaini* [1980]), *Burial Ground* (*Le notti del terrore*; a.k.a *Night of Terror* [1980]), *Zombie Holocaust* (*Zombi Holocaust* [1980]), and *Hell of the Living Dead* (*Virus: L'inferno dei morti viventi*; a.k.a. *Night of the Zombies* [1980]), *Oasis of the Zombies* (*L'abime des morts vivants; La tumba de los muertos vivientes* [1982]), *Revenge of the Dead* (*Zeder* [1983]), *Killing Birds* (*Uccelli assassini* [1987]), *Rest in Pieces* (*Descanse en piezas* [1987]), *After Death* (*Oltre la morte* [1988]), and *Zombie 3* (*Zombi 3* [1988]).

Fulci, meanwhile, followed *Zombie* with a series of unconventional zombie-filled horror films—a loose triad of surrealist works known as the *Gates of Hell* trilogy. In *City of the Living Dead* (*Paura nella citta dei morti viventi* [1980]), *The Beyond* (*. . . E tu vivrai nel terrore! L'aldilà* [1981]), and *The House by the Cemetery* (*Quella villa accanto al cimitero* [1981]), Fulci renounced conventional narrative structure to conjure fragmented, nightmarish visuals beyond the terrors of hell.

In the United States, a record number of zombie films also went into production during the 1980s, but the Hollywood mainstream remained averse to the living-dead frenzy. As in decades past, the glut of films were mostly B-grade, green-lit by independents, producing such eclectic titles as *Toxic Zombies* (1980), *Dead & Buried* (1981), *Alien Dead* (1980), *Battalion of the Living Dead* (1981), *Curse of the Screaming Dead* (1982), *I Was a Zombie for the FBI* (1982), *One Dark Night* (1983), *Hard Rock Zombies* (1985), *Deadly Friend* (1986), *Gore-Met*

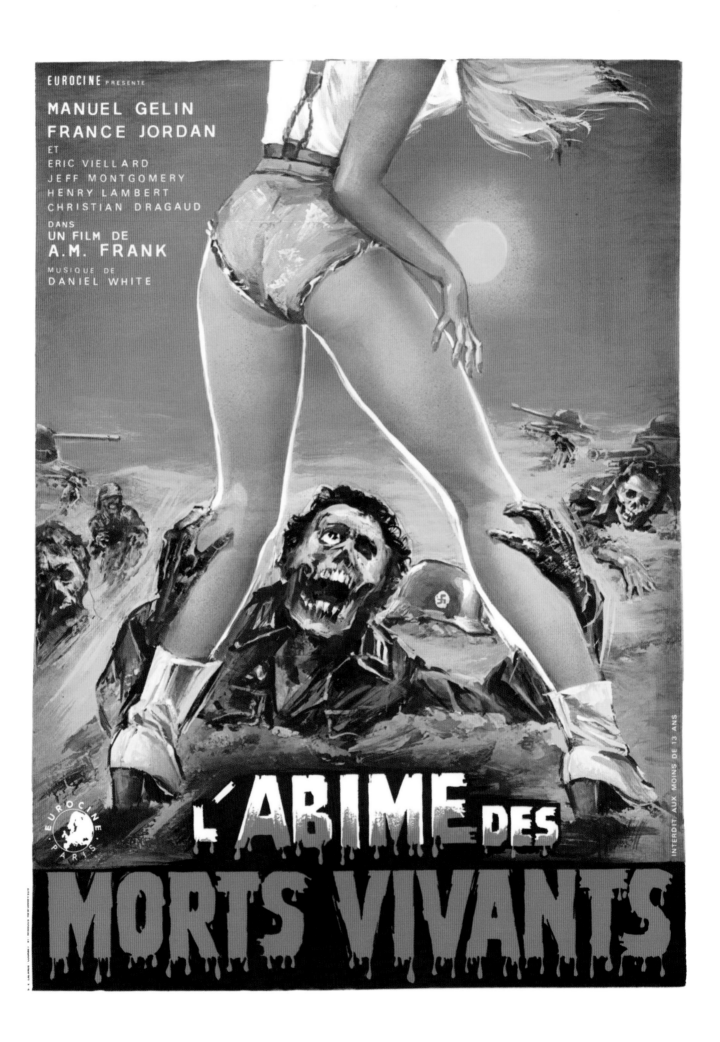

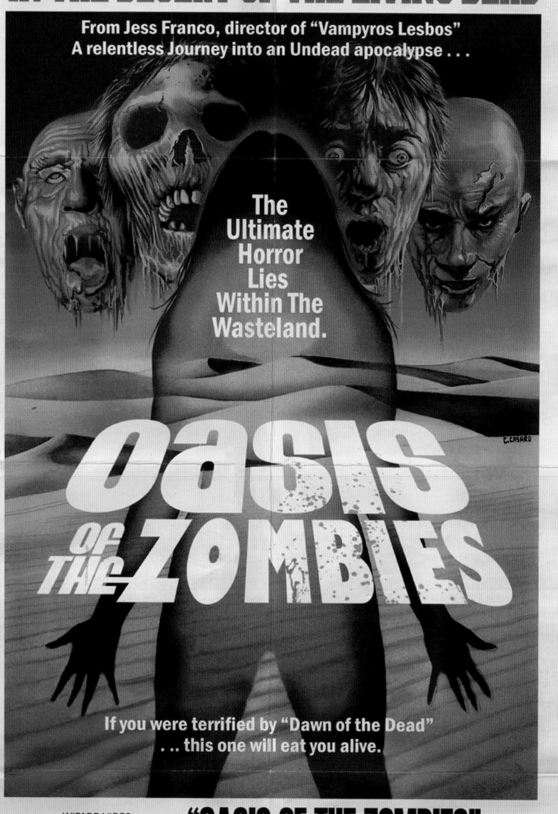

Left: American movie poster for *Oasis of the Zombies* (*L'abime des morts vivants*; *La tumba de los muertos vivientes*).

Opposite: Posters for the American releases of *Burial Ground* (*Le notti del terrore*; a.k.a *Night of Terror* [1980]) (top left); Fulci's *The Gates of Hell* (a.k.a. *City of the Living Dead* (*Paura nella citta dei morti viventi* [1980]) (top right); *Nightmare City* (*Incubosulla citta contaminata* [1980]) (bottom left); and *Revenge of the Dead* (*Zeder* [1983]) (bottom right).

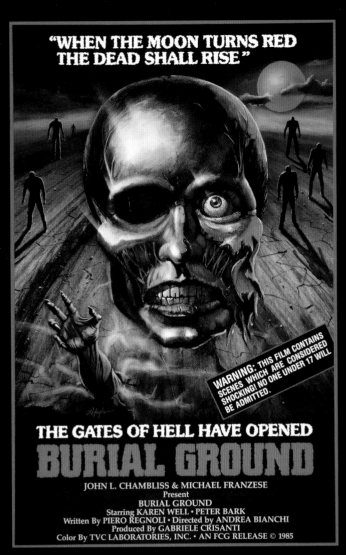

"WHEN THE MOON TURNS RED
THE DEAD SHALL RISE"

WARNING: THIS FILM CONTAINS
SCENES WHICH ARE CONSIDERED
SHOCKING! NO ONE UNDER 17 WILL
BE ADMITTED.

THE GATES OF HELL HAVE OPENED

BURIAL GROUND

JOHN L. CHAMBLISS & MICHAEL FRANZESE
Present
BURIAL GROUND
Starring KAREN WELL • PETER BARK
Written By PIERO REGNOLI • Directed by ANDREA BIANCHI
Produced By GABRIELE CRISANTI
Color By TVC LABORATORIES, INC. • AN FCG RELEASE © 1985

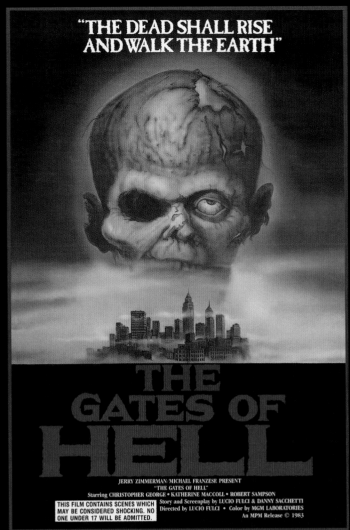

"THE DEAD SHALL RISE
AND WALK THE EARTH"

THE
GATES OF
HELL

JERRY ZIMMERMAN/MICHAEL FRANZESE PRESENT
"THE GATES OF HELL"
Starring CHRISTOPHER GEORGE • KATHERINE MACCOLL • ROBERT SAMPSON
Story and Screenplay by LUCIO FULCI & DANNY SACCHETTI
Directed by LUCIO FULCI • Color by MGM LABORATORIES
THIS FILM CONTAINS SCENES WHICH
MAY BE CONSIDERED SHOCKING. NO
ONE UNDER 17 WILL ADMITTED.
An MPM Release © 1983

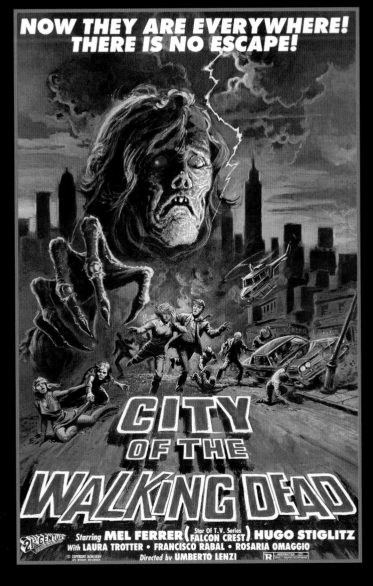

NOW THEY ARE EVERYWHERE!
THERE IS NO ESCAPE!

CITY
OF THE
WALKING DEAD

Starring MEL FERRER (Star Of T.V. Series FALCON CREST) HUGO STIGLITZ
With LAURA TROTTER • FRANCISCO RABAL • ROSARIA OMAGGIO
Directed by UMBERTO LENZI

"THE DEAD SHALL RISE"

REVENGE
OF THE
DEAD

MOTION PICTURE MARKETING
PRESENTS
"REVENGE OF THE DEAD"
Starring JOHN STACY • ANN CANOVAS • GABRIEL LAVIA
A Film By PUPI AVATI • Director of Photography FRANK COLLI

THIS FILM CONTAINS SCENES WHICH
MAY BE CONSIDERED SHOCKING. NO
ONE UNDER 17 WILL BE ADMITTED.

Prints by
GETTY FILM LABORATORIES
AN MPM RELEASE © 1984

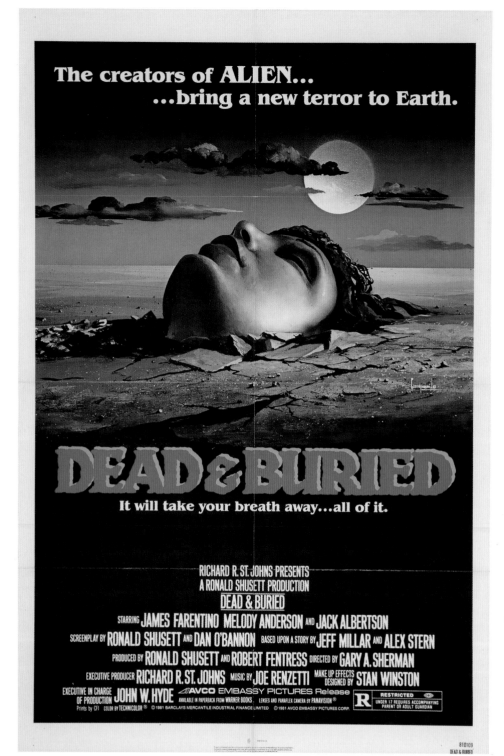

The creators of ALIEN...
...bring a new terror to Earth.

DEAD & BURIED

It will take your breath away...all of it.

RICHARD R. ST. JOHNS PRESENTS
A RONALD SHUSETT PRODUCTION
DEAD & BURIED
STARRING JAMES FARENTINO MELODY ANDERSON AND JACK ALBERTSON
SCREENPLAY BY RONALD SHUSETT AND DAN O'BANNON BASED UPON A STORY BY JEFF MILLAR AND ALEX STERN
PRODUCED BY RONALD SHUSETT AND ROBERT FENTRESS DIRECTED BY GARY A. SHERMAN
EXECUTIVE PRODUCER RICHARD R. ST. JOHNS MUSIC BY JOE RENZETTI MAKE UP EFFECTS DESIGNED BY STAN WINSTON
EXECUTIVE IN CHARGE OF PRODUCTION JOHN W. HYDE AVCO EMBASSY PICTURES Release
AVAILABLE IN PAPERBACK FROM WARNER BOOKS LENSES AND PANAFLEX CAMERA BY PANAVISION
Prints by CFI COLOR BY TECHNICOLOR © 1981 BARCLAYS MERCANTILE INDUSTRIAL FINANCE LIMITED © 1981 AVCO EMBASSY PICTURES CORP.
R RESTRICTED UNDER 17 REQUIRES ACCOMPANYING PARENT OR ADULT GUARDIAN

810109
DEAD & BURIED

il nuovo film di LUCIO FULCI

PAURA
NELLA CITTA' DEI
MORTI VIVENTI

CHRISTOPHER GEORGE · KATHERINE MAC COLL · CARLO DE MEJO
ANTONELLA INTERLENGHI · GIOVANNI LOMBARDO RADICE
DANIELA DORIA · FABRIZIO JOVINE · e con JANET AGREN nel ruolo di SANDRA
Fotografia SERGIO SALVATI · Musiche FABIO FRIZZI · Colore LV LUCIANO VITTORI
Regia di LUCIO FULCI
Produzione DANIA FILM · MEDUSA DISTRIBUZIONE · NATIONAL CINEMATOGRAFICA

Above: Film poster for *Alien* (1979) screenwriters Ronald Shusett and Dan O'Bannon's *Dead & Buried* (1981), and Italian poster for Fulci's *City of the Living Dead* (*Paura nella citta dei morti viventi* [1980]) (right).

Opposite: Out from the weeds come *Toxic Zombies* (1980).

Zombie Chef from Hell (1986), *House* (1986), *Neon Maniacs* (1986), *Night of the Creeps* (1986), *Raiders of the Living Dead* (1986), *The Supernaturals* (1986), *Zombiethon* (1986), *I Was a Teenage Zombie* (1987), *Redneck Zombies* (1987), *The Video Dead* (1987), *Zombie Death House* (1987), *Zombie High* (1987), *Dead Heat* (1988), *The Dead Next Door* (1988), *Ghost Town* (1988), *Beverly Hills Bodysnatchers* (1989), *Chopper Chicks in Zombietown* (1989), *The Chilling* (1989), *Dead Pit* (1989), *The Laughing Dead* (1989), *Night Life* (1989), and *The Vineyard* (1989). A few managed to rise up into cult status, generating a series of sequels in an already saturated market.

Ten years after Amicus's horror anthology *Tales from the Crypt* (1972), director Romero and noted horror author Stephen King combined their creative efforts and love of 1950s EC Comics to create their own 1980s anthology, *Creepshow* (1982). Eschewing the apocalyptic themes of Romero's *Dead* films for comic-book morality tales, this nostalgic throwback was billed as "The Most Fun You'll Have Being Scared!" The five segments are tied together with animated interstitials that give it a classic comic-book feel. The ensemble cast includes Hal Holbrook, Leslie Nielsen, E. G. Marshall, and an early cameo by Ed Harris. Romero drafted his *Dawn of the Dead* (1978) special makeup effects guru Tom Savini to

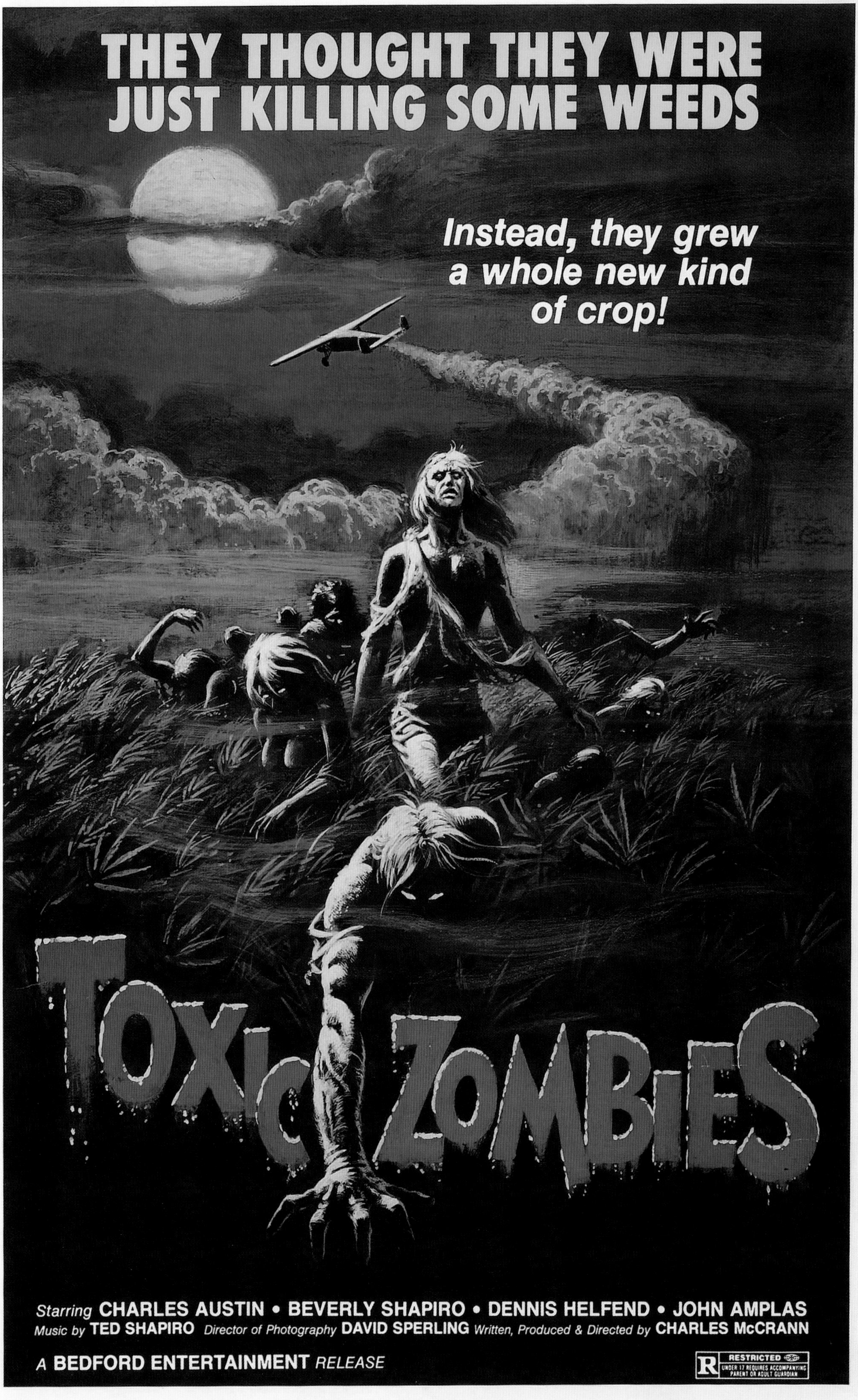
THEY THOUGHT THEY WERE
JUST KILLING SOME WEEDS
Instead, they grew
a whole new kind
of crop!
TOXIC ZOMBIES
Starring CHARLES AUSTIN • BEVERLY SHAPIRO • DENNIS HELFEND • JOHN AMPLAS
Music by TED SHAPIRO Director of Photography DAVID SPERLING Written, Produced & Directed by CHARLES McCRANN
A BEDFORD ENTERTAINMENT RELEASE
R RESTRICTED
UNDER 17 REQUIRES ACCOMPANYING
PARENT OR ADULT GUARDIAN

The Masters Of Terror And The Macabre
GEORGE A. ROMERO   STEPHEN KING
Director of "Night of the Living Dead" and   Author of "Carrie," "The Shining," "The Stand,"
"Dawn of the Dead."   "Firestarter," and "Cujo."

CREEPSHOW

The Most Fun You'll Ever Have BEING SCARED!

ADMISSION
•ADULTS
•CHILDREN

ADMIT 1

Starring HAL HOLBROOK • ADRIENNE BARBEAU • FRITZ WEAVER • LESLIE NIELSEN
CARRIE NYE • E.G. MARSHALL and VIVECA LINDFORS as Aunt Bedelia

A LAUREL PRODUCTION "CREEPSHOW." A GEORGE A. ROMERO FILM

Production Design CLETUS ANDERSON   Makeup Special Effects TOM SAVINI   Director of Photography MICHAEL GORNICK   Associate Producer DAVID E. VOGEL

Executive Producer SALAH M. HASSANEIN   Original Screenplay STEPHEN KING   Produced by RICHARD P. RUBINSTEIN   Directed by GEORGE A. ROMERO

820155
CREEP SHOW

create the more traditional scares. Warner Bros. picked up the film and distributed it widely to favorable reception, eventually garnering a comic-book adaptation, a sequel, *Creepshow 2* (1987), and the direct-to-video *Creepshow III* (2006).

Before breaking into the mainstream with the *Spider-Man* trilogy (*Spider-Man* [2002], *Spider-Man 2* [2004], *Spider-Man 3* [2007]), and Disney's *Oz the Great and Powerful* (2013), director Sam Raimi cut his teeth on the $90,000 independent splatter-fest *The Evil Dead* (1981). While Raimi's cult classic, and its two sequels, *Evil Dead II* (1987) and *Army of Darkness* (1993), are not strictly zombie films, the reanimated, demon-possessed corpses, known as Deadites, have left an indelible impression on the subgenre. Since its debut, the original series has successfully expanded into a cross-platform franchise, with comic books, toys, and video games, and even inspiring a musical. Ironically, distributors initially dismissed the low-budget thriller, until it found a champion in author Stephen King, who, after catching it at an Out of Competition screening at the Cannes Film Festival, hailed it as "the most ferociously original horror film of 1982." The story centers on a group of youths who unwittingly summon dormant demons to their remote cabin in the woods. But it was the film's sardonic tone and audacious style King was referring to that made the series distinctive and memorable. Raimi combined splatter with slapstick comedy to create an over-the-top visceral symphony of revoltingly outrageous physical gags put on display for a single unapologetic purpose—to make the audience shriek. By the third installment a decade later, Raimi was pitting his unlikely hero Ash (Bruce Campbell) and his "boom-stick," against an entire army of Deadites in the Middle Ages.

Above: Director George A. Romero and writer Stephen King on the set of *Creepshow*.

Opposite: Theatrical poster for *Creepshow* (1982), a nostalgic homage to EC Comics.

Above: Film poster for writer–director
Sam Raimi's *The Evil Dead* (1981).

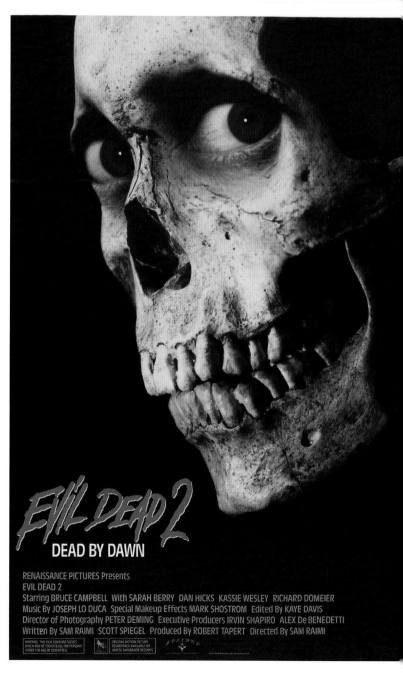

Top: Annie (Sarah Berry), Jake (Dan Hicks), Ash (Bruce Campbell), Bobby Joe (Kassie Wesley) prepare for splatter in *Evil Dead II* (1987) (left); Ash (Campbell) fights off the Deadites in *Army of Darkness* (1993) (right).

Above: Poster for *Army of Darkness*, the third installment in the *Evil Dead* series.

Right: Poster for *Evil Dead II*.

Overleaf: Raimi's skeletal tribute to Ray Harryhausen's stop-motion animation, *Army of Darkness*.

By the early 1980s, the living dead had been terrorizing cinemagoers in low-budget films for fifty years, and they had become synonymous with the B movies they populated. While zombie films remained a guilty pleasure for a large segment of the public, they still lacked mainstream acceptance, and their contributions to pop culture went unrecognized. But one fateful pairing would begin to change all of that. On December 2, 1983, the undead underdogs of the horror genre were exhumed from cult status to mainstream prominence when director John Landis and international recording artist Michael Jackson wrote them into their landmark musical short film, *Thriller* (1983).

Initially, when Jackson's album *Thriller* went on sale in the fall of 1982, there were no plans to release a single, let alone a music video for the spooky title track. Instead, those distinctions went to the tracks "Billie Jean" and "Beat It," huge hits that had finally begun to break down the racial barrier on MTV—the nascent cable music television network that had a reputation for not airing videos from black artists. Although the *Thriller* album had been successful, by the summer of 1983 it began losing its footing at the top of the Billboard charts, and Jackson was unhappy.

Opposite: Ash (Bruce Campbell) wields his weapon of choice in a publicity photo for *The Evil Dead* (1981).

Above: Michael Jackson poses with his troop of dancing zombies for director John Landis's musical short, *Thriller* (1983).

Right: Michael Jackson's *Thriller* (1983) rocketed zombies into the global pop-cultural mainstream.

Right: Michael Jackson's *Thriller* (1983) rocketed zombies into the global pop-cultural mainstream.

Below: Bub the zombie (Sherman Howard) jams to music on a Walkman in *Day of the Dead* (1985).

Opposite: Film poster for *Day of the Dead*.

Overleaf: The dead unite against the living in *Day of the Dead*.

When his record label suggested releasing a third music video for the title track, Jackson approached feature film director John Landis after seeing his horror comedy *An American Werewolf in London* (1981). The director had also found commercial success with the musical comedy *The Blues Brothers* (1980). Landis pitched Jackson a narrative short film adaptation of the song, to be shot on 35mm film with high-end production values that could be released theatrically. The nostalgic throwback to 1950s and '60s horror movies would deliver fun chills, incorporating dialogue and Vincent Price's haunting soliloquy as Jackson led a troop of zombies in a riveting synchronized dance sequence. Rick Baker, Landis's Academy Award–winning special makeup effects artist from *An American Werewolf in London*, designed and created the ghastly ghouls that rise out of their graves.

When the budget came in at $500,000 ("Billie Jean's" video's budget was considered high at $250,000) the record label scoffed at the amount, a much higher cost than most of the living dead's feature-length films. But the King of Pop's dancing zombies had a powerful front man, and Jackson offered to underwrite the film himself. Eventually, producers devised a way to raise the funds by pre-selling the fourteen-minute musical short, packaging it with a forty-five-minute behind-the-scenes documentary, *Making Michael Jackson's Thriller* (1983). "We sold that hour to a brand-new thing called cable television and the Showtime network. They paid a quarter of a million dollars for the rights to show it exclusively for, I think, ten days," recalled Landis. "MTV went crazy—'How can you do that?' We said, 'OK, you give us money.' And they gave us another quarter of a million to show it for two weeks, and that was our costs." MTV's world-premiere video won two Grammy Awards, four MTV Awards, a People's Choice Award, and went on to revolutionize the music industry. *Thriller* appealed to all audiences and crossed cultural barriers, becoming a global pop-cultural sensation. And Jackson's album rode the wave back to the top of the charts a year after its release, becoming the most successful album of all time. In 2009, the Library of Congress recognized *Thriller*'s cultural impact, a first for a music video, inducting it into the National Film Registry, where it joined its zombie predecessor *Night of the Living Dead* (1968).

For his part, Romero continued his apocalyptic *Dead* series with the follow-up *Day of the Dead* (1985). By this third installment, he has completely turned the tables. While the dead overrun the surface of the globe, the living have been driven underground. From a subterranean government facility in Florida, a small team mostly made up of scientists and military men search for a solution to the zombie epidemic. Romero's social commentary about the living's lack of civility is even more apparent in *Day of the Dead* through his depictions of unlikable survivors and sympathetic flesh-eaters. Zombies in *Day of the Dead* are nabbed and held as captive specimens, while the film's eccentric scientist, nicknamed "Frankenstein"

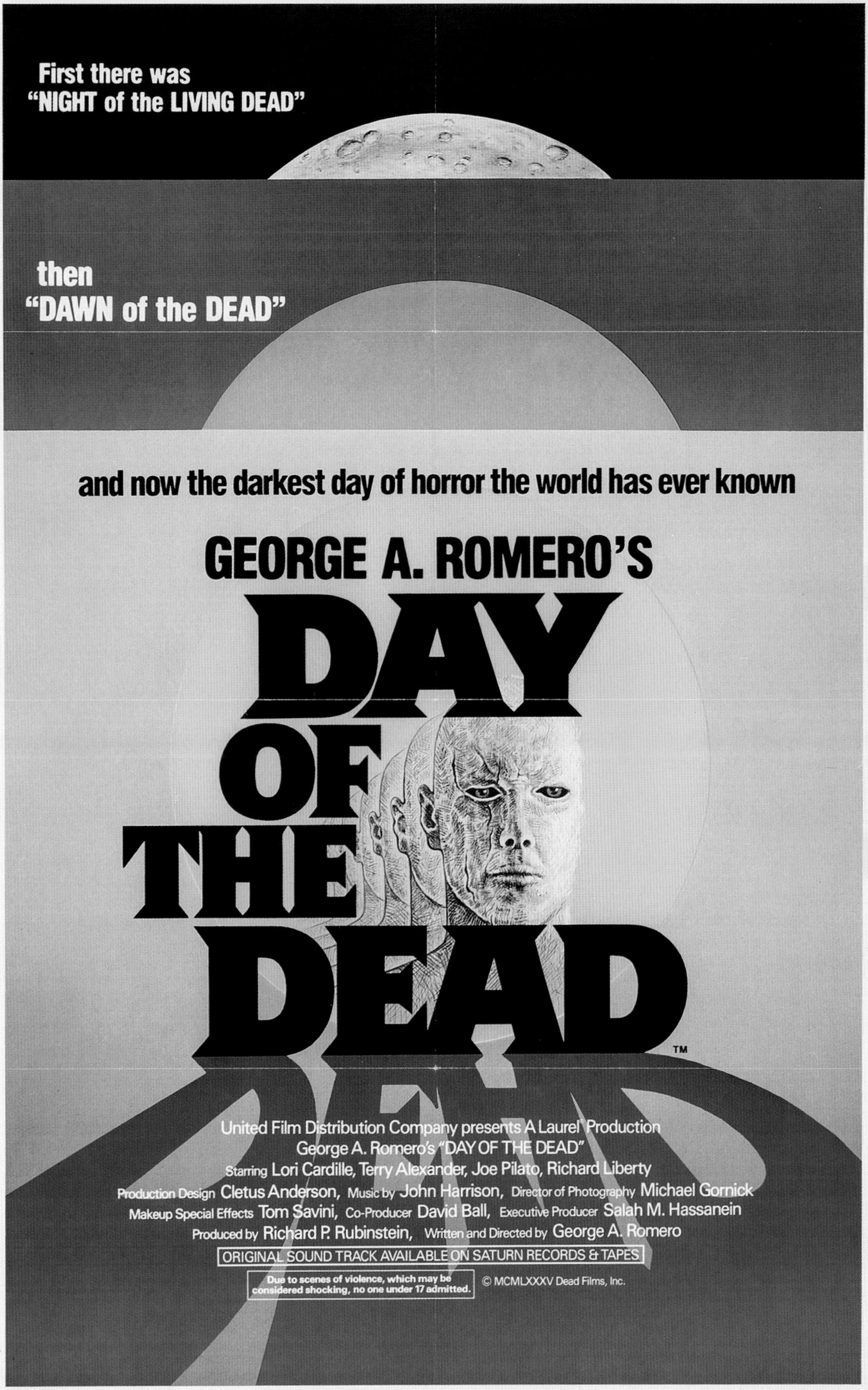
First there was
"NIGHT of the LIVING DEAD"
then
"DAWN of the DEAD"
and now the darkest day of horror the world has ever known
GEORGE A. ROMERO'S
DAY OF THE DEAD
TM
United Film Distribution Company presents A Laurel Production
George A. Romero's "DAY OF THE DEAD"
Starring Lori Cardille, Terry Alexander, Joe Pilato, Richard Liberty
Production Design Cletus Anderson, Music by John Harrison, Director of Photography Michael Gornick
Makeup Special Effects Tom Savini, Co-Producer David Ball, Executive Producer Salah M. Hassanein
Produced by Richard P. Rubinstein, Written and Directed by George A. Romero
ORIGINAL SOUND TRACK AVAILABLE ON SATURN RECORDS & TAPES
Due to scenes of violence, which may be considered shocking, no one under 17 admitted.
© MCMLXXXV Dead Films, Inc.

DAY OF THE DEAD

(Richard Liberty), conducts gruesome experiments on them. The mad doctor even discovers how to domesticate one of his zombie test subjects, training the mute ghoul like a seal and naming him Bub. Played for sympathy by actor Sherman Howard, Bub gradually regains a sort of childlike awareness, along with certain motor skills, eventually "remembering" how to use a firearm. By the film's finale, the viewer is rooting for the zombies over the military goons, who are ultimately torn in half and devoured by the dead. The grisly makeup effects gags are distinguished, courtesy once again of Tom Savini. The picture also focuses on finding the cause of the outbreak, more so than the previous two films. John (Terry Alexander), the group's heroic Caribbean helicopter pilot, attempts to give headstrong scientist Dr. Sarah Bowman (Lori Cardille) a supernatural perspective: "You want to put some kinda explanation down here before you leave? Here's one as good as any you're likely to find—we've been punished by the Creator. He visited a curse on us so we might get a look at what Hell was like. Maybe He didn't want to see us blow ourselves up, and put a big hole in His sky. Maybe He just wanted to show us He was still the boss man. Maybe He figured we was getting too big for our britches trying to figure His shit out."

While *Day of the Dead*'s zombie metaphors certainly made it a fitting companion to Romero's first two *Dead* pictures, by the mid-1980s, audiences preferred to see the dead return in more upbeat and fun popcorn fare, rather than in social melodramas. Four weeks after *Day of the Dead*'s theatrical release, young audiences flocked to see Orion Pictures' splatter-spoof *Return of the Living Dead* (1985)—a landmark in the subgenre for introducing brain-eating zombies. The punk-age parody that touted, "They're back from the grave and ready to party!" tripled the domestic box-office take of *Day of the Dead*, became a cult classic on home video and cable, and spawned four sequels: *Return of the Living Dead Part II* (1988), *Return of the Living Dead 3* (1993), *Return of the Living Dead: Necropolis* (2005), and *Return of the Living Dead: Rave to the Grave* (2005).

Above: Bub the zombie (Sherman Howard) gradually recovers sense memory.

Opposite: Sarah's (Lori Cardille) nightmares are realized in a Japanese poster for *Day of the Dead*.

Above: Ernie (Don Calfa) and Spider (Miguel Nuñez) examine the inexplicable in *Return of the Living Dead* (1985).

Opposite: Film poster for Dan O'Bannon's punk-rock zombie-farce, *Return of the Living Dead*, initially based on a story by the screenwriter of *Night of the Living Dead* (1968), John A. Russo.

Return of the Living Dead began as a 1978 novelized sequel to *Night of the Living Dead*, written by Romero's co-writer on the classic film, John A. Russo, after the two screenwriters had amicably parted ways. Russo began development of a film version with director Tobe Hooper (*The Texas Chain Saw Massacre* [1974]) that was based on his straight-forward horror book. But when screen-writer Dan O'Bannon (*Alien* [1979]) was brought on board for rewrites, the tone of the picture began to shift. Eventually, when Hooper left to pursue another project, O'Bannon took over the directing reins, turning Russo's story into a zombie parody about two workers in a medical supply warehouse who tamper with mis-placed army drums and unleash the brain-eating dead. Frank (James Karen) asks his young trainee (Thom Matthews), "Did you see that movie *Night of the Living Dead*? . . . Did you know that movie was based on a true case?" Apparently, it stemmed from a chemical spill at the Pittsburgh VA hospital, when the army's experimental "245 Trioxin" leaked down into the morgue and made all the dead bodies come to life. As Frank tells it, "They told the guy who made the movie that if he told the true story, they'd just swoop his ass off. So he changed all the facts around." The military kept it a secret, but when they shut down the operation and shipped out all the contaminated dirt and bodies, the transportation department got the orders crossed and sent them to the medical supply warehouse. "Wanna see 'em?" offers Frank. Pretty soon, one of the drums ruptures, and the two men, along with warehouse owner Burt (Clu Gulager) and a group of teenage punks, must deal with the zombie mayhem that ensues.

Also from the independent scene came two twistedly wicked zombie-themed films that became cult hits due to their popularity as video rentals—the sci-fi-leaning *Re-Animator* (1985), and the action-slasher film *Maniac Cop* (1988). Written and directed by Stuart Gordon, and based on H. P. Lovecraft's short story "Herbert West–Reanimator" (1922), the outrageously gory horror comedy stars Jeffrey Combs as West, a mad scientist who stops at nothing in his efforts to reanimate the dead. Two sequels followed: *Bride of Re-Animator* (1990) and *Beyond Re-Animator* (2003). In *Maniac Cop*, written by Larry Cohen and directed by William B. Lustig, a serial killer on a murder spree in New York City turns out to be an

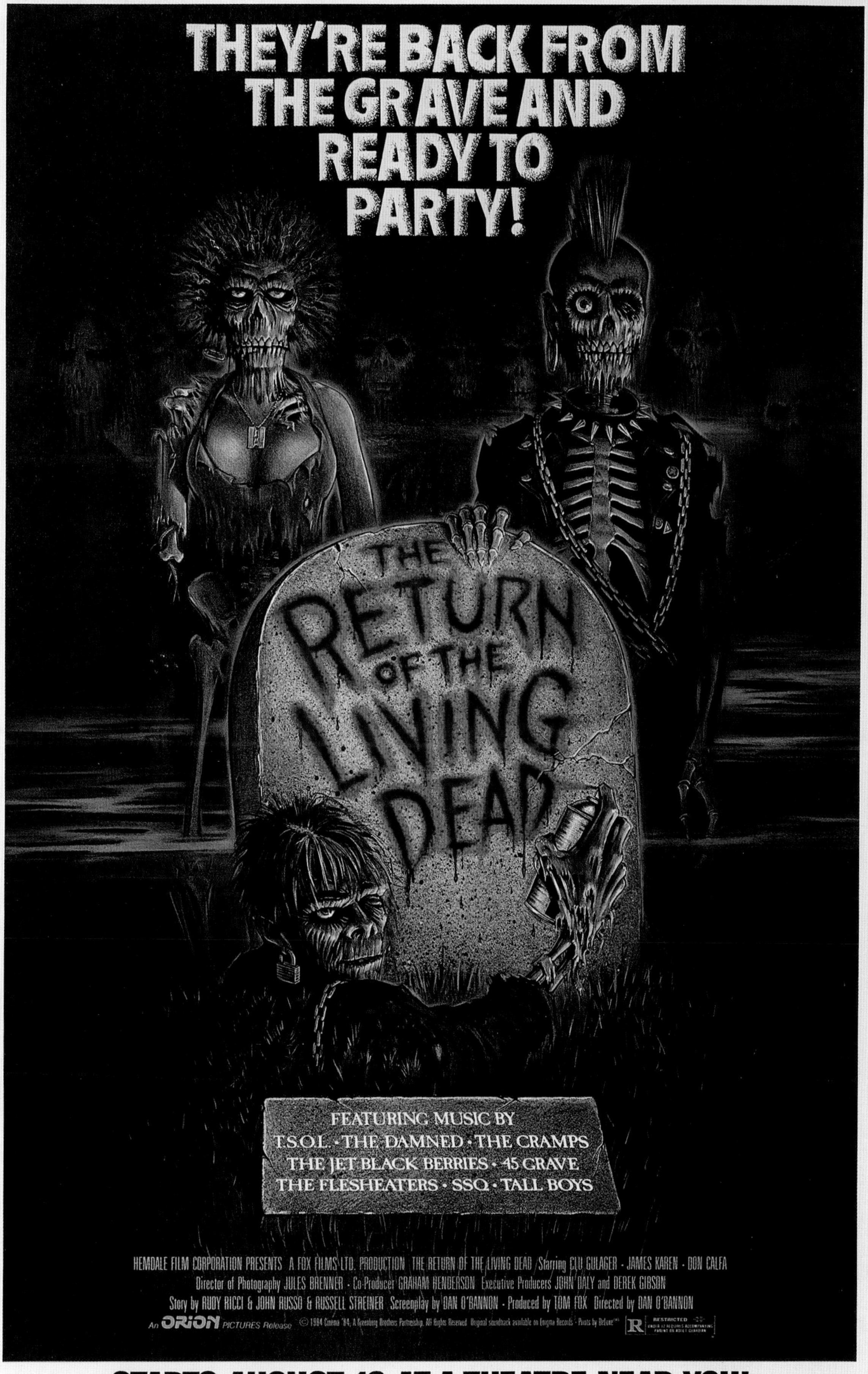

STARTS AUGUST 16 AT A THEATRE NEAR YOU!

Above: Director Stuart Gordon's *Re-Animator* (1985).

Right: Release poster for the sequel *Bride of Re-Animator* (1990) (top); Japanese poster for *Re-Animator* (bottom).

Opposite: Dr. Carl Hill (David Gale) loses his head with Herbert West (Jeffrey Combs) in *Re-Animator* (top); West (Combs) admires his reanimated creation (Kathleen Kinmont) in *Bride of Re-Animator* (bottom).

YOU HAVE THE RIGHT TO REMAIN SILENT...
FOREVER.

MANIAC
COP

GLICKENHAUS FILMS, INC. PRESENTS A LARRY COHEN PRODUCTION A WILLIAM LUSTIG FILM "MANIAC COP"
STARRING TOM ATKINS • BRUCE CAMPBELL • LAURENE LANDON • RICHARD ROUNDTREE
WILLIAM SMITH • ROBERT Z'DAR AND SHEREE NORTH MUSIC BY JAY CHATTAWAY
CO-PRODUCER JEF RICHARD EXECUTIVE PRODUCER JAMES GLICKENHAUS PRODUCED BY LARRY COHEN DIRECTED BY WILLIAM LUSTIG
© 1987 SHAPIRO/GLICKENHAUS FILMS, INC.   RECORDED IN ULTRA·STEREO

infamous NYPD officer back from the dead. Subsequent follow-ups were *Maniac Cop 2* (1990) and *Maniac Cop III: Badge of Silence* (1993).

While mainstream Hollywood avoided producing splatter, there were a couple of zombie-related pictures that came out of the studio system toward the end of the decade. Both were based on previously published works: Wade Davis's 1985 nonfictional investigative novella, *The Serpent and the Rainbow: A Harvard Scientist's Astonishing Journey into the Secret Societies of Haitian Voodoo, Zombies, and Magic* (1985), and Stephen King's *Pet Sematary* (1983). Director Wes Craven (*A Nightmare on Elm Street* [1984]) helmed a relatively credible adaptation of Davis's book for Universal Pictures, exploring Haiti's zombie origins. *The Serpent and the Rainbow* (1988) stars Bill Pullman as ethnobotanist Dennis Alan, who travels to Haiti to uncover the secret voodoo brew behind zombism, and is buried alive by the Tonton Macoute. The following year, Paramount Pictures released *Pet Sematary* (1989), helmed by top music-video director Mary Lambert. King wrote the screenplay based on his horror tale about a pet cemetery (its sign eerily misspelled in the book) that can bring the dead back to life, albeit with dire consequences for a desperate family man. While both films did modest business, the latter producing the sequel, *Pet Sematary Two* (1992), as the 1980s drew to a close, the zombie subgenre seemed to be exhausted. It's as if all the splatter had dried up the well of interest and creativity. At no other time had there been that many zombie films released into the market, and by decade's end audiences seemed fatigued and ready to move on. But the dead have a way of coming back.

Above: NYPD officer Matt Cordell (Robert Z'Dar) is a vengeful, undead *Maniac Cop* (1988).

Opposite: Movie poster for Larry Cohen and William Lustig's *Maniac Cop*.

Opposite Top and Bottom Left: Victor Pascow (Brad Greenquist) gives some advice to Louis Creed (Dale Midkiff) in *Pet Sematary* (1983).

Above, Right, and Opposite Bottom Right: *The Serpent and the Rainbow* (1988), starring Bill Pullman.

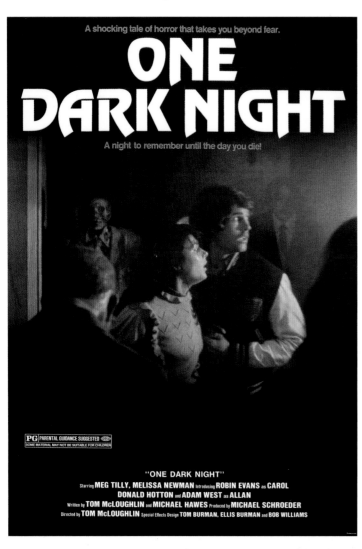

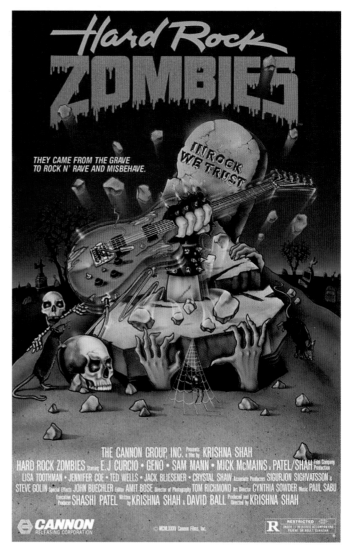

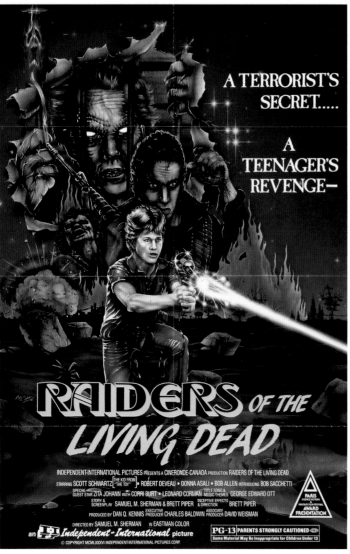

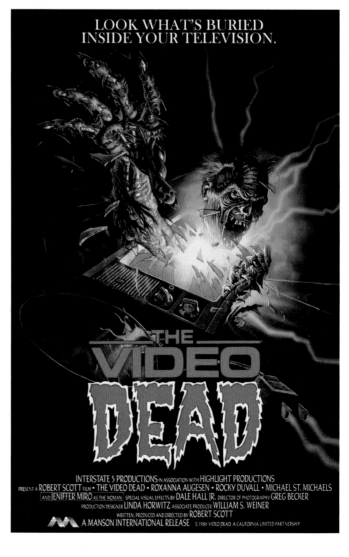

Opposite: Posters for the zombie-themed B movies *One Dark Night* (1983) (top left); *Hard Rock Zombies* (1985) (top right); *Raiders of the Living Dead* (1986) (bottom left); and *The Video Dead* (1987) (bottom right).

Above: Film poster for the horror-comedy *House* (1986).

Above: Poster for the ultra-low-budget Troma release *Redneck Zombies* (1987).

Opposite: Movie posters for the low-budget zombie outings *Ghost Town* (1988) (top left); *Night of the Creeps* (1986) (top right); *The Chilling* (1989) (bottom left); and *Chopper Chicks in Zombietown* (1989) (bottom right).

The good. The bad. The Satanic.

GHOST·TOWN

EMPIRE PICTURES Presents A CHARLES BAND PRODUCTION "GHOST TOWN"
Starring FRANK LUZ JIMMIE F. SKAGGS CATHERINE HICKLAND BRUCE GLOVER
MICHAEL ALLDREDGE Music by HARVEY R. COHEN Editors PETER TESCHNER & KING WILDER
Director of Photography MAC AHLBERG Executive in Charge of Production FRANK HILDEBRAND
Executive Producer CHARLES BAND Story by DAVID SCHMOELLER Screenplay by DUKE SANDEFUR
Produced by TIMOTHY D. TENNANT Directed by RICHARD GOVERNOR

"The good news is your dates are here.
The bad news is...they're dead."

NIGHT OF THE CREEPS

If you scream...you're dead.

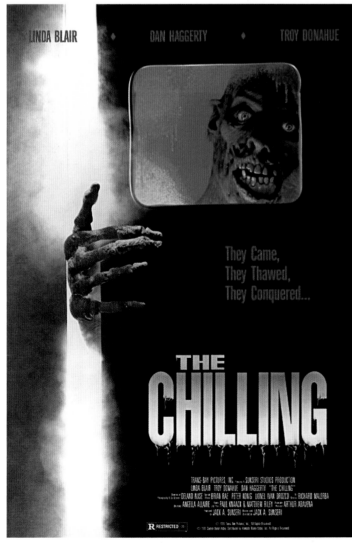

LINDA BLAIR   DAN HAGGERTY   TROY DONAHUE

They Came,
They Thawed,
They Conquered...

THE CHILLING

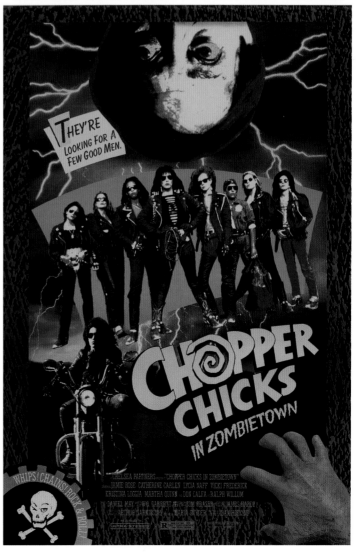

THEY'RE LOOKING FOR A FEW GOOD MEN.

CHOPPER CHICKS IN ZOMBIETOWN

Some things won't stay down...
even after they die.

DEAD·ALIVE

TIMOTHY BALME · DIANA PEÑALVER · ELIZABETH MOODY · IAN WATKIN "DEAD ALIVE" PROSTHETICS DESIGN BOB McCARRON CREATURE & GORE EFFECTS RICHARD TAYLOR PRODUCTION DESIGN KEVIN LEONARD-JONES
MUSIC PETER DASENT DIRECTOR OF PHOTOGRAPHY MURRAY MILNE EDITOR JAMIE SELKIRK SCREENPLAY STEPHEN SINCLAIR FRANCES WALSH PETER JACKSON
PRODUCER JIM BOOTH DIRECTOR PETER JACKSON

DOLBY STEREO®
IN SELECTED THEATRES

A WINGNUT FILMS PRODUCTION © 1992

TRIMARK PICTURES

Due to the SHOCKING NATURE of this film, NO ONE UNDER 17 ADMITTED

THE [VIDEO]GAME

CHANGER

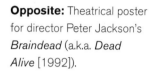

y the 1990s, it seemed as if cinema had explored and exploited all dramatic possibilities for the living dead. For approximately sixty years, filmmakers had produced an eclectic mix of zombie-themed horror films with a wide range of styles and budgets, from melodramas and comedies to action and science fiction, musicals, and even parodies. As the century was winding down, the historical high levels of zombie films released in the 1980s had dwindled to a historical low. The few that surfaced in the early 1990s seemed like vestiges from the prior decade of zombie excess.

In *Dead Men Don't Die* (1990), Elliott Gould stars as a news anchorman who is killed by gangsters and brought back from the dead as a zany zombie. Before being nominated for an Academy Award for producing director Robert Altman's period ensemble mystery, *Gosford Park* (2001), Bob Balaban directed *My Boyfriend's Back* (1993). Referencing the 1963 song by The Angels, the romantic comedy that "proves true love never dies" tells the story of teen Johnny Dingle (Andrew Lowery), who returns from the grave to date his high school crush (Traci Lind). Appearing in small roles early in their careers are Philip Seymour Hoffman, Matthew McConaughey, and Matthew Fox. The Italian/French/German coproduction titled *Cemetery Man* (*Dellamorte Dellamore* [1994]) stars Rupert Everett as a cemetery caretaker who defends the small town of Buffalora from zombies. Based on Tiziano Sclavi's Italian graphic novel series *Dylan Dog* (1986), the source material was adapted again years later for the U.S. production *Dylan Dog: Dead of Night* (2011), starring Brandon Routh.

One of the last blasts of zombie splatter-slapstick came from a most unlikely hobbit in Middle-earth. Approximately nine years before Peter Jackson released his first feature-film adaptation of J. R. R. Tolkien's magnum opus *The Lord of the Rings* (1954), the Academy Award–winning filmmaker directed the outrageous horror-comedy *Braindead* (a.k.a. *Dead Alive* [1992]). The estimated $1.8 million-dollar gore-fest, financed by a grant from the New Zealand Film Commission, was Jackson's third feature film and it was highly influenced by the works of Raimi and Romero. Jackson once declared, "*Braindead* is nothing more than a zombie fan just going crazy wanting to make a zombie movie, you know? A lot of the stuff I do and continue to do, really, is based on just being a fan of certain things." The inventive gags are so gory that splatter-master Lucio Fulci is even said to have declared them over-the-top. Written by Jackson, Fran Walsh, and Stephen Sinclair, it tells the story of Lionel Cosgrove (Timothy Balme) and his overbearing mum (Elizabeth Moody), who falls ill and dies after being bitten by a "Sumatran rat-monkey." She soon comes back to life as a flesh-eating zombie, eating a pet dog and killing and infecting her nurse and neighbors. Lionel does his best to cover up and contain the situation at home, but to save the day, he must eventually confront his beastly

Opposite: Theatrical poster for director Peter Jackson's *Braindead* (a.k.a. *Dead Alive* [1992]).

Below: Poster for 1993's *My Boyfriend's Back*.

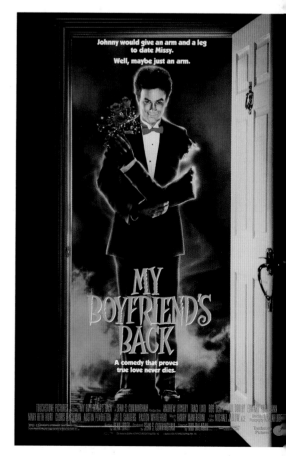

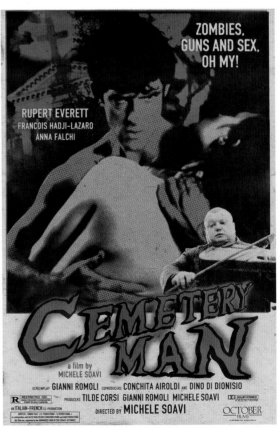

This page: Rupert Everett (with Anna Falchi) in *Cemetery Man* (*Dellamorte Dellamore* [1994]).

Opposite: Poster for *Braindead* (a.k.a. *Dead Alive*).

BRAINDEAD

TIMOTHY BALME   DIANA PEÑALVER   ELIZABETH MOODY   IAN WATKIN

PROSTHETICS DESIGN **BOB McCARRON**   CREATURE & GORE EFFECTS **RICHARD TAYLOR**   PRODUCTION DESIGN **KEVIN LEONARD-JONES**

MUSIC **PETER DASENT**   DIRECTOR OF PHOTOGRAPHY **MURRAY MILNE**   EDITOR **JAMIE SELKIRK**

SCREENPLAY **STEPHEN SINCLAIR   FRANCES WALSH   PETER JACKSON**

PRODUCER **JIM BOOTH**   DIRECTOR **PETER JACKSON**

ORO FILMS

A WINGNUT FILMS PRODUCTION

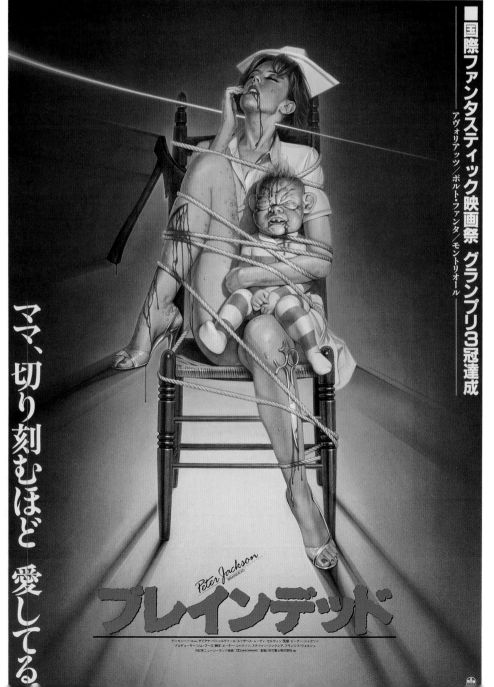

Peter Jackson

Above: Lionel Cosgrove (Timothy Balme) is forced to confront his domineering mother, his insecurities, and zombies in *Braindead* (a.k.a. *Dead Alive*).

Left: Japanese poster for *Braindead* (a.k.a. *Dead Alive*) featuring artwork by Hajime Sorayama.

Opposite: Peter Jackson directs the gore on the set of *Braindead* (a.k.a. *Dead Alive*).

Above: Lionel struggles to break free of the chokehold his mother has on him in *Braindead* (a.k.a. *Dead Alive*).

Opposite: Columbia Pictures and George A. Romero attempt to revive the dead by remaking the classic.

mother. "Stephen Sinclair, who co-wrote the script, he'd devised the story of *Braindead* as a stage play," recalled Jackson. "Stephen was very focused on wanting to satirize New Zealand society, and he loved the idea of the dark events that are happening behind the drawn curtains." He explained, "In every house when the curtains are drawn, there's a story going on and you never get to hear. You get the public side of things, the happy, smiling, social activities. But really, you know, you peel that layer away and what darkness dwells in the suburbs." Although *Braindead* was well received by critics and won numerous awards on the film festival circuit, the picture's weak box-office performance seemed to reflect audiences' waning interest in the subgenre.

By the late twentieth century, the living dead had become victims of their overexposure. They were now perceived as banal caricatures, no longer intriguing or effective at terrifying cinemagoers. Many hoped that a modern, color remake of Romero's masterpiece, also titled *Night of the Living Dead* (1990), would reignite the subgenre, as the original once did. But the sociopolitical climate and the independent spirit that forged the original film became impossible to recapture twenty years later. For this go-round, Romero brought back some of the core crew from the original, and tapped his special makeup effects wizard Savini to direct. While the reported $4.2-million-dollar production cost afforded the latest advancements in special effects, it also tied the filmmakers to the mainstream Hollywood studio Columbia Pictures and their rated-R release requirements. It became apparent that the actual reason for the remake was strictly a financial one. "The reason we did the remake is a long, involved, more legal story than a creative one," admitted Romero. "We made the [original] film, threw it in the trunk of the car, and took it to New York to see if anyone would want to show this to people, and they did. It went out and it became *Night of the Living Dead*. But no one ever made any money, none of our group." The reason: *Night of the Living Dead* had entered the public domain. Before the classic was released theatrically in 1968, the film's original distributor, The Walter Reade Organization, had gone back into Romero's print of the film to change the title. As Romero recalled, "One day, somebody discovered that there was no copyright on the film, because our original title was *Night of the Flesh Eaters*, and we, stupidly, as young filmmakers, put the copyright bug—the

This spread: Patricia Tallman, Bill Mosley, and Greg Funk re-create the classic.

Overleaf: Ben (Tony Todd) resists the Night of the Living Dead (1990).

little 'c' with the circle around it—on the title card. And when they changed the title that bug came off, and all of the sudden there was no copyright. They didn't notice. We didn't notice. Nobody noticed. All of the sudden, there was no copyright on the film. So the moment that people realized that, everybody was selling it on VHS. . . . Everybody could release it without having to pay any royalties or anything else."

The remake also afforded Romero, who wrote the updated version, an opportunity to repair what he felt was his unjust characterization of the female protagonist in the original film. "Back in 1968, the character of Barbara was probably, well, unfortunately typical of the kind of female characters that were in movies those days, and I probably didn't give her enough credit or make her a strong enough person. So, in this one I wanted to make her strong from the get-go, and that was probably the biggest change." That doesn't mean that Romero gave the film a complete overhaul. Aware of the audience's current apathy toward modern-day zombies, he asserted, "We were really not trying to fit it into the '90s. If it was really going to be a '90s version, people wouldn't care, you know? Zombies would walk down the street and everyone would just say, 'Uh, another one of those guys.'" And that's exactly what happened. Reception from both audiences and critics was lackluster, and verified what many already suspected. The zombie film craze that had begun in 1968 with Night of the Living Dead had come to a definitive conclusion with the film's remake, just over twenty years later.

While zombies had all but vanished from movies by the mid-1990s, their presence was being felt in a more interactive media platform, video games. In 1994, Japanese video-game developer and publisher Capcom tapped game designer Shinji Mikami to create an adult horror title for the new Sony PlayStation and Sega Saturn consoles. "I wanted to do a real scary game, not ghosts or crap like that, but real monsters that you could see and would come and attack," remarked Mikami. Partly inspired by Romero's Living Dead film series and Fulci's Zombie (Zombi 2 [1979]), the young designer and his team created the template for what

Capcom marketing eventually coined the "survival horror" genre—games specifically designed to shock and scare a player by placing their vulnerable alter egos in horrific environments with limited inventory, and where the object is surviving. Released in March of 1996, the game bore the title *Biohazard* in Japan, but Capcom changed it for North America and Europe, where it was known as *Resident Evil*. The game became a critical and financial sensation, selling 2.75 million units worldwide, and singlehandedly launched *Resident Evil* as a cross-platform franchise that would eventually encompass multiple game sequels, movies, comic books, and toys. Comparable "survival horror " games eventually followed, and although it would still take a few years for zombies to return to American multiplexes, one film from Hong Kong heralded their forthcoming resurgence. In director Wilson Yip's horror-comedy *Bio-Zombie* (*Sun faa sau si* [1998]), a group of retail store employees fight through a zombie outbreak at the mall. While the loose premise spoofs Romero's *Dawn of the Dead* (1978), Yip retooled the concept, infusing the film with visual gags and graphics referencing contemporary zombie video-game culture and young heroes that evoke the slackers from Kevin Smith's *Clerks* (1994) and *Mallrats* (1995).

On the heels of Capcom's enormous hit, *Resident Evil* (a.k.a. *Biohazard*), the video-game giant diligently prepped a highly anticipated follow-up game. Prior to launch in 1998, the Japanese video-game maker hired Romero to bring their hit game to life in a $1.5-million-dollar live-action commercial. The man responsible for conceiving the modern-day zombie seemed to relish the assignment: "I loved making the movies, and it's great that there's a game which is, you know, it's like a flashback to that genre. I can feel maybe a little bit like I had some influence on it, and so I feel very flattered." The spot for *Resident Evil 2* (a.k.a. *Biohazard 2* [1998]), which aired exclusively in Japan, starred Brad Renfro and Adrienne Frantz, and was produced like a feature film, according to Romero. "We wanted it to look like a movie, so we basically wanted to produce it very much like a movie

This page: Rolls (Angela Tong) (top), and Crazy Bee (Sam Lee) (bottom) in *Bio-Zombie* (*Sun faa sau si* [1998]).

Opposite: Crazy Bee (Lee), Woody Invincible (Jordan Chan), and Rolls (Tong).

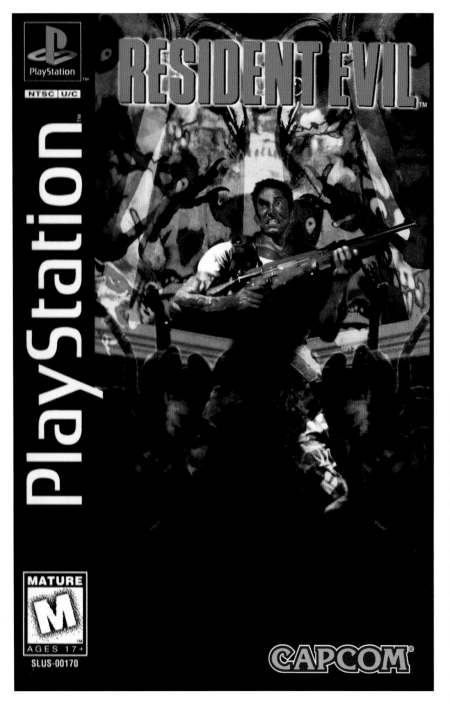

Above: Box art for video game designer Shinji Mikame's landmark game-changer from Capcom, *Resident Evil* (a.k.a. *Biohazard* [1996]).

Opposite: Japanese flyer for *Resident Evil* (a.k.a. *Biohazard*).

instead of like a commercial shoot. It was just like a small motion-picture shoot with extras playing the zombies, and a few people that were experienced playing the zombies." The Japanese-born Hollywood special makeup effects artist Screaming Mad George designed the creatures with pronounced facial features and rotting flesh, but held back on the gore due to the commercial's intended mainstream audience. Capcom was reportedly extremely pleased with Romero's work, and when word broke outside of Japan about the existence of the commercial, so did speculation regarding the zombie filmmaker's potential involvement in an eventual feature film adaptation of *Resident Evil*.

Prior to their collaboration with Romero on the commercial, Capcom had already licensed off the *Resident Evil* film rights to Constantin Film. The German production company, which had previously distributed Romero's *Dawn of the Dead* (1978) across Germany with much success, was already on friendly terms with the filmmaker. A strong endorsement from Capcom sealed the deal, and Romero was hired to write the feature-length adaptation with an opportunity to direct. "I had written a script for *Resident Evil* that I liked, and that Capcom liked, but then [Constantin Film] just said, 'That's not what we want to do.'" Romero acknowledged his disappointment in a personal blog entry years later while discussing unrealized projects: "But the *biggest* damn shame was *Resident Evil*. We busted balls writing drafts of that screenplay. I'm talkin' marathons, seventy-two hours straight. I really wanted this project. I had directed a TV commercial for *ResEv II*, and being on the set again with zombies (by Screamin' Mad George), I was hooked. Deep in my heart, I felt that *ResEv* was a rip-off of *Night of the Living Dead*. I had no legal case, but I was resentful. And torn . . . because I liked the video game. I wanted to do the film partly because I wanted to say, '*Look here! This is how you do this shit!*'" But Constantin had a different vision for *Resident Evil*, and the film stalled in development until after the turn of the new century, when it would become the first big-budget studio zombie movie in the subgenre's history.

MILLA JOVOVICH   MICHELLE RODRIGUEZ

RESIDENT EVIL

SURVIVE THE HORROR

SCREEN GEMS/CONSTANTIN FILM/DAVIS FILMS PRESENT A CONSTANTIN FILM/NEW LEGACY FILM/DAVIS FILMS PRODUCTION IN ASSOCIATION WITH IMPACT PICTURES
A FILM BY PAUL W.S. ANDERSON STARRING: MILLA JOVOVICH MICHELLE RODRIGUEZ ERIC MABIUS "RESIDENT EVIL" JAMES PUREFOY MARTIN CREWES COLIN SALMON
DIRECTOR OF PHOTOGRAPHY DAVID JOHNSON, BSC PRODUCTION AND COSTUME DESIGNER RICHARD BRIDGLAND VISUAL EFFECTS SUPERVISOR RICHARD YURICICH, ASC EDITOR ALEXANDER BERNER MUSIC SUPERVISOR LIZ GALLACHER
ORIGINAL SCORE BY MARCO BELTRAMI AND MARILYN MANSON PRODUCTION EXECUTIVE CHRISTINE ROTHE CO-PRODUCER CHRIS SYMES EXECUTIVE PRODUCERS ROBERT KULZER VICTOR HADIDA DANIEL KLETZKY YOSHIKI OKAMOTO
BASED UPON CAPCOM'S VIDEOGAME "RESIDENT EVIL" PRODUCED BY BERND EICHINGER SAMUEL HADIDA JEREMY BOLT PAUL W.S. ANDERSON WRITTEN AND DIRECTED BY PAUL W.S. ANDERSON

SUPPORTED BY filmboard. FFA-- filmförderungsfonds Bayern

SOUNDTRACK ON ROADRUNNER RECORDS FEATURING NEW MUSIC FROM SLIPKNOT

Constantin Film   DAVIS FILMS   DOLBY DIGITAL

www.Resident-Evil-The-Movie.com

8 ZOMBIE

ZEITGEIST

The dead began their rise to mainstream prominence at the dawn of the twenty-first century in the Land of the Rising Sun. Japan's homegrown video-game series *Resident Evil* (a.k.a. *Biohazard*) seemed to spark the imagination of local filmmakers, who began producing the next-generation of zombie-themed content. A crop of films invaded the market, mashing 1980s splatter-slapstick, martial arts, manga comics, and the living dead in movies such as the rock 'n' roll zombie invasion blowout *Wild Zero* (1999); the Yakuza-versus-zombies heist picture *Junk* (*Shiryo-gari* [2000]); the kinetic supernatural horror-fantasy *Versus* (2000), which pits gangsters, guns, and swordplay against vengeful zombies; *Stacy: Attack of the Schoolgirl Zombies* (*Stacy* [2001]), in which young girls ages fifteen to seventeen begin dying and reawakening as zombies; and *Battlefield Baseball* (*Jigoku Koshien* [2003]), a bizarre comedy that fuses Japan's love of baseball with the living dead.

By mid-2001, *Variety* announced that Sony's Columbia TriStar was acquiring the North American distribution rights to Constantin Film's upcoming *Resident Evil* (2002). The motion-picture adaptation of Capcom's best-selling video game, with its estimated $33-million-dollar budget, was the most expensive zombie-themed film to date, and one of the most high profile. Following their creative differences with Romero, Constantin had hired Paul W. S. Anderson (*Mortal Kombat* [1995]) to write and direct the movie they wanted: a slick, mainstream blockbuster franchise. Much to the dismay of some hardcore horror and game fans, Anderson's film focused more on action than gore, and instead of a literal adaptation of the video game, it expanded the game universe with original characters. He cast Milla Jovovich as the amnesiac heroine Alice, who joins forces with an elite military unit to contain a virus outbreak and destroy an out-of-control supercomputer and its flesh-eating staff of scientists. The apocalyptic finale sees Alice awaken to a deserted Raccoon City, where an old newspaper comes into view, headline exclaiming: "THE DEAD WALK!"—a tip of the hat to a similar moment from Romero's *Day of the Dead* (1985). Although *Resident Evil* lacked critical enthusiasm upon its release, the young demographic that the filmmakers hoped would fill seats, did. The movie grossed over $102 million dollars worldwide, and its commercial success launched the subgenre's first billion-dollar film franchise, with a series of live-action installments that followed: *Resident Evil: Apocalypse* (2004), *Resident Evil: Extinction* (2007), *Resident Evil: Afterlife* (2010), *Resident Evil: Retribution* (2012), and a sixth film set for release in 2015. Capcom and Sony Pictures also teamed to produce two full-length computer-animated features, *Resident Evil: Degeneration* (2008), and *Resident Evil: Damnation* (2012), which were released on home video and other platforms.

Opposite: Theatrical poster for director Paul W. S. Anderson's film adaptation of *Resident Evil* (2002).

Below: Poster for the Yakuza-versus-zombies Japanese picture *Junk* (*Shiryo-gari* [2000]).

Above: J.D. (Pasquale Aleardi) and Rain (Michelle Rodriguez) are engulfed by zombies in *Resident Evil* (2002).

Left: Actor Jaymes Butler in full zombie makeup in *Resident Evil*.

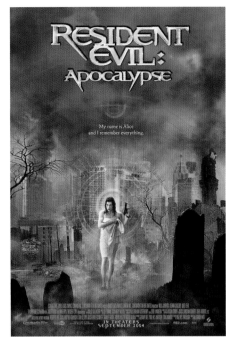

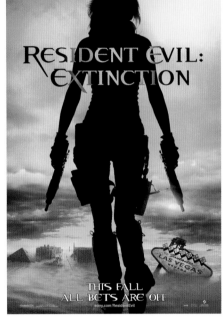

Left: Milla Jovovich reprises her role as Alice in *Resident Evil: Apocalypse* (2004) (top), and in *Resident Evil: Extinction* (2007) (middle and bottom).

Above: Posters for the second and third film in the series.

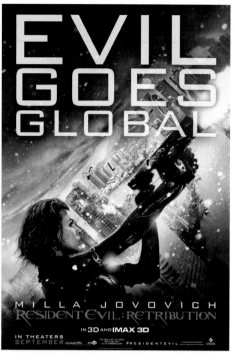

Above: Theatrical posters for *Resident Evil: Afterlife* (2010) (left), and *Resident Evil: Retribution* (2012) (middle); Jovovich's Alice is a mainstay in the franchise (right) as is director Paul W. S. Anderson, on the set of *Resident Evil: Afterlife* (bottom).

Opposite: Zombies attempt to break into prison in *Resident Evil: Afterlife* (top); Alice (Jovovich) combats the infected flesh-eaters in *Resident Evil: Retribution* (bottom).

Overleaf: Alice (Jovovich) takes aim in *Resident Evil: Afterlife*.

Above: Writer Alex Garland and director Danny Boyle deploy an infected, rage-filled populace on Jim (Cillian Murphy) after he awakens *28 Days Later* (2002).

Opposite: Poster art for *28 Days Later*.

Just a few months after the first *Resident Evil* was released theatrically to huge fanfare, a much lower-budget post-apocalyptic horror film, shot on digital video with a cast of relative unknowns, made its way to screens in the United Kingdom. *28 Days Later* (2002), from English screenwriter Alex Garland and future Academy Award–winning director for *Slumdog Millionaire* (2008), Danny Boyle, depicts with devastating credibility the dissolution of society following a viral epidemic. Actor Cillian Murphy portrays Jim, a bicycle courier who awakens from a coma in an abandoned London hospital. After wandering the streets of the seemingly deserted English capital, he makes the startling discovery that a highly contagious psychological virus has infected the population. These rage-filled, fast-moving aggressors are not reanimated corpses, and therefore not considered zombies by many genre purists. In fact, director Boyle has maintained that he never envisioned the rage-filled creatures in *28 Days Later* to be part of any zombie lineage, but when Romero's "ghouls" first debuted in *Night of the Living Dead* (1968), neither did he. Whether intentional or not, the fact remains: like the ghouls in Romero's classic, *28 Days Later* became an influential part of the evolution of zombies on film. The indie horror movie was lauded by critics and audiences alike, becoming a hit, earning $82 million dollars at the worldwide box office, and spawning the successful sequel, *28 Weeks Later* (2007).

Following the success of *28 Days Later*, Hollywood's most preeminent studio during horror's heyday was finally willing to welcome the zombie into their stable of classic monsters. In 2004, Universal Pictures green-lit director Zack Snyder's $28- million-dollar modern-day adaptation of *Dawn of the Dead* (2004). While Romero had no involvement in the film's production, writer James Gunn's (*Guardians of the Galaxy* [2014]) screenplay employs the same basic premise as

FROM THE DIRECTOR OF TRAINSPOTTING & THE BEACH

DANNY BOYLE
REINVENTS THE
ZOMBIE
HORROR
FILM AND IT'S
"SCARY
AS HELL"
DAILY MAIL

28
DAYS
LATER

YOUR DAYS ARE NUMBERED
6·27·03
WWW.28DAYSLATER.COM

WHEN THERE'S NO MORE ROOM IN HELL,
THE DEAD WILL WALK THE EARTH.

DAWN OF THE DEAD

UNIVERSAL PICTURES PRESENTS A STRIKE ENTERTAINMENT/NEW AMSTERDAM ENTERTAINMENT PRODUCTION "DAWN OF THE DEAD" SARAH POLLEY VING RHAMES JAKE WEBER AND MEKHI PHIFER
MUSIC TYLER BATES MUSIC SUPERVISOR G. MARQ ROSWELL EDITOR NIVEN HOWIE PRODUCTION DESIGNER ANDREW NESKOROMNY DIRECTOR OF PHOTOGRAPHY MATTHEW F. LEONETTI ASC EXECUTIVE PRODUCERS THOMAS A. BLISS DENNIS E. JONES ARMYAN BERNSTEIN
www.dawnofthedeadmovie.net PRODUCED BY RICHARD P. RUBINSTEIN MARC ABRAHAM ERIC NEWMAN BASED ON A SCREENPLAY BY GEORGE A. ROMERO SCREENPLAY BY JAMES GUNN DIRECTED BY ZACK SNYDER

STRIKE | THIS FILM IS NOT YET RATED   **COMING SOON**   A UNIVERSAL PICTURE UNIVERSAL
© 2004 UNIVERSAL STUDIOS

the original, being about a group of survivors holed up in a shopping mall in the midst of a zombie invasion. The film, however, ditches Romero's sociopolitical wit and sub-context and features running zombies akin to those in *28 Days* Later—a source of contention for Romero. "Partially, it's a matter of taste," he once told a reporter. "I remember Christopher Lee's mummy movies where there was this big old lumbering thing that was just walking towards you and you could blow it full of holes but it would keep coming. And in the original *Halloween* (1978), Michael Meyers never ran—he just sort of calmly walked across the lawn or across the room. To me, that's scarier: this inexorable thing coming at you and you can't figure out how to stop it. Aside from that," he explained, "I do have rules in my head of what's logical and what's not. I don't think zombies can run. Their ankles would snap!" Critic Roger Ebert, an admirer of the original *Dawn of the Dead*, wrote in his positive review of the remake, that comparisons are "instructive in the ways that Hollywood has grown more skillful and less daring over the years. From a technical point of view, the new *Dawn of the Dead* is slicker and more polished, and the acting is better, too. But it lacks the mordant humor of the Romero version, and although both films are mostly set inside a shopping mall, only Romero uses that as an occasion for satirical jabs at a consumer society." Snyder's feature film directorial debut managed to adhere to an R rating, and effectively delivered the scares, gore, and action to satiate mainstream audiences and garner $102 million in global ticket sales. *Dawn of the Dead*'s success eventually encouraged remakes based on Romero's other works, with *Day of the Dead* (2008) and *The Crazies* (2010) following later in the decade.

Above: Running zombies take to the streets in *Dawn of the Dead* (2004).

Opposite: Theatrical poster for director Zack Snyder's remake of George A. Romero's original.

Opposite: Ana (Sarah Polley) and Kenneth (Ving Rhames) confront the zombie horde in *Dawn of the Dead*.

Above: Michael (Jake Weber), Ana (Sarah Polley), Andre (Meki Phifer), and a pregnant Luda (Inna Korobkina) find refuge inside a shopping mall in *Dawn of the Dead*.

Above: A zombie apocalypse (top) provokes Shaun (Simon Pegg) to win back his girlfriend Liz (Kate Ashfield) (bottom) in *Shaun of the Dead* (2004).

Opposite: Film poster for Simon Pegg and Edgar Wright's "zom rom com," *Shaun of the Dead.*

Overleaf: English zombies amass in *Shaun of the Dead.*

Just as the successive box-office hits *Resident Evil, 28 Days Later,* and *Dawn of the Dead* ushered in a new generation of filmmakers who had retooled Romero's zombie precepts for millennial audiences, a pair of young English filmmakers offered another variation on the theme, but without altering Romero's canon. *Shaun of the Dead* (2004), the self-described "zom rom com," or zombie romantic comedy, was co-written by director Edgar Wright and Simon Pegg as a scary yet satirical old-school homage to Romero's *Dead* series. Pegg also stars as Shaun, a slacker electronics store employee who is roused by a zombie apocalypse to grow up, repair his life, and win back his girlfriend. The popular British film received rave reviews from critics, but it was Romero's enthusiastic endorsement that Wright and Pegg, die-hard fans, cherished above all. Romero returned the favor by making their dreams come true, and casting them as featured zombie extras in *Land of the Dead* (2005).

At sixty-four years old, Romero returned to the genre that he reinvented, and for the first time he had the backing of a mainstream Hollywood studio. Ironically, after producing a profitable remake based on Romero's classic *Dawn of the Dead* (1978), Universal Pictures gave the independent-spirited writer-director approximately $15 million dollars to make *Land of the Dead*, the fourth installment in his living dead oeuvre. But the partnership with a big studio meant that Romero would have to make certain creative compromises with Universal executives. "I had this convention, I had used African American leads in all of the dead movies. I wrote the character again as an African American," recalled Romero. "Universal wouldn't let it happen." They were concerned about the picture's commercial viability abroad, said the writer-director to a panel of fans, paraphrasing for the studio: "'We have to sell Europe, and Europe doesn't buy African American leads unless it's Denzel [Washington].'" So as a result, Romero made the lead zombie a black man. He recalled thinking: "You won't let me make [the character] Riley black?

A Romantic Comedy.
With Zombies.
SHAUN OF THE DEAD
KATE ASHFIELD LUCY DAVIS NICK FROST DYLAN MORAN BILL NIGHY PENELOPE WILTON
RONALDO VASCONCELLOS ANNIE HARDINGE MARCUS ROWLAND CHRIS DICKENS DAVID M. DUNLAP TIM BEVAN ERIC FELLNER
NATASCHA WHARTON JAMES WILSON ALISON OWEN SIMON PEGG AND EDGAR WRIGHT NIRA PARK EDGAR WRIGHT
R RESTRICTED
For Zombie Violence/Gore And Language
www.shaunofthedeadmovie.com
STUDIO CANAL
ROGUE PICTURES
This September aim for the head.
"AN ABSOLUTE BLAST!"
~George Romero

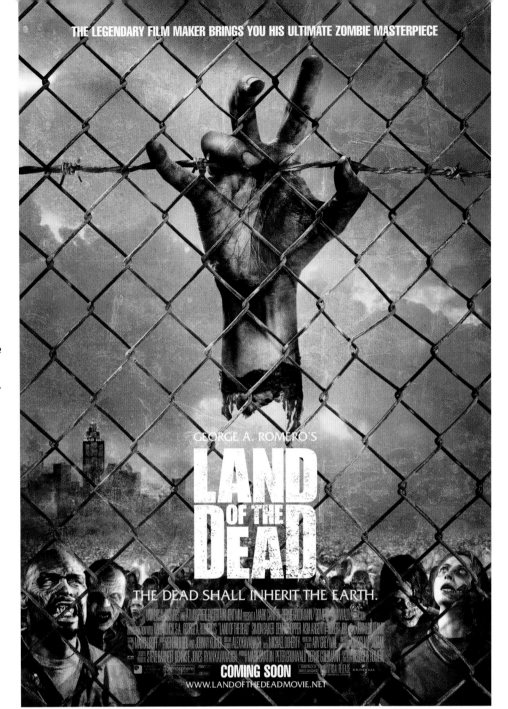

GEORGE A. ROMERO'S

LAND OF THE DEAD

THE DEAD SHALL INHERIT THE EARTH.

COMING SOON
WWW.LANDOFTHEDEADMOVIE.NET

Well, then Big Daddy's going to be black, and he's going to kick ass!" The character of Big Daddy (Eugene Clark) is, in many respects, a direct descendant of the zombie Bub from *Day of the Dead* (1985)—an intuitive and empathetic zombie the audience can root for.

Romero's signature sociopolitical voice did remain intact, and his critical observations about class conflict in America became a central theme in *Land of the Dead*. As Manohla Dargis observed in her *New York Times* review, "One of the enormous pleasures of genre filmmaking is watching great directors push against form and predictability, as Mr. Romero does brilliantly in *Land of the Dead*." True to his previous *Dead* films, Romero remained critical about the living, illustrating how, in a post-apocalyptic world overrun by zombies, society's survivors have devolved into a divided class system between the haves and the have-nots, rather than banding together against a common enemy. In contrast, the zombies do seem to be evolving, and uniting, in a massive assault against the living.

Romero followed *Land of the Dead* with a pair of modern-day zombie films that are disconnected from his chronological quartet of *Dead* pictures. *Diary of the Dead* (2007) and its sequel, *Survival of the Dead* (2009), returned Romero to his independent film roots, and represented the start of a new series and new characters. "I wanted to go back to lower budgets," said the director. "I wanted to do something about citizen journalism and the emerging media and all of that." Although it has a contemporary setting, *Diary of the Dead* resets the events to the first days of the zombie outbreak, following a small group of young filmmakers who record the widespread epidemic in documentary style. "I thought that would be a one-off, my little statement about what journalism is becoming today. Because it was so inexpensive to make, and even though it had a limited release, that film wound up making a lot of money and so everybody said, 'Let's do it again.'" With *Survival of the Dead*, Romero subverted the Western genre, taking a page from William Wyler's *The Big Country* (1958) and adding zombies. A small band of rogue soldiers looking for safe haven wind up on Plum Island, a fishing and ranching outpost off the coast of New England, where they find themselves caught between two feuding families who disagree on whether to contain the zombies until a cure is found, or wipe them out all together.

Above: Poster for *Land of the Dead* (2005), the fourth installment in Romero's series.

Opposite: Big Daddy (Eugene Clark) unites the dead against the living in *Land of the Dead*.

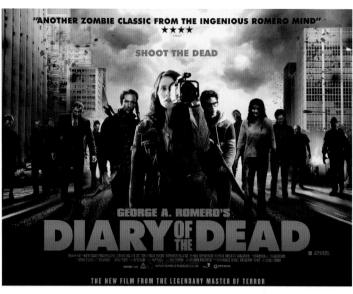

Above: Poster art for Romero's *Diary of the Dead* (2007) (top), and *Survival of the Dead* (2009) (bottom).

Right: Big Daddy (Eugene Clark) leads an attack (top); John Leguizamo watches Romero set up a shot in *Land of the Dead* (bottom).

Opposite: Gordo (Chris Violette) watches Eliot (Joe Dinicol) skewer a zombie in *Diary of the Dead* (top); Jane (Kathleen Munroe) snaps at Chuck (Joris Jarsky) in *Survival of the Dead* (bottom).

Overleaf: Jason (Joshua Close) rolls on Ridley (Philip Riccio) in *Diary of the Dead.*

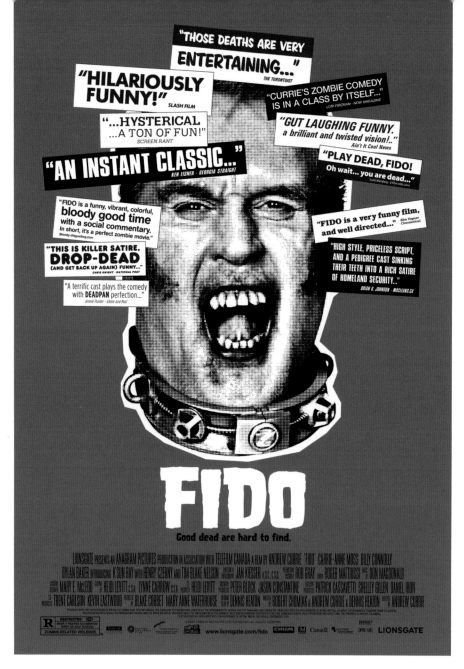

"THOSE DEATHS ARE VERY ENTERTAINING..." THE TORONTOIST

"HILARIOUSLY FUNNY!" SLASH FILM

"CURRIE'S ZOMBIE COMEDY IS IN A CLASS BY ITSELF..." LORI FIREMAN - NOW MAGAZINE

"...HYSTERICAL ...A TON OF FUN!" SCREEN RANT

"GUT LAUGHING FUNNY. a brilliant and twisted vision!.." Ain't It Cool News

"AN INSTANT CLASSIC..." KEN EISNER - GEORGIA STRAIGHT

"PLAY DEAD, FIDO! Oh wait... you are dead..." Scott Weinberg - EFilm.com

"FIDO is a funny, vibrant, colorful, bloody good time with a social commentary. In short, it's a perfect zombie movie." Bloody-disgusting.com

"FIDO is a very funny film, and well directed..." Kim Voynar Cinematical

"THIS IS KILLER SATIRE, DROP-DEAD (AND GET BACK UP AGAIN) FUNNY..." CHRIS KNIGHT - NATIONAL POST

"HIGH STYLE, PRICELESS SCRIPT, AND A PEDIGREE CAST SINKING THEIR TEETH INTO A RICH SATIRE OF HOMELAND SECURITY..." BRIAN D. JOHNSON - MACLEANS.CA

"A terrific cast plays the comedy with DEADPAN perfection..." Jennie Punter - Globe and Mail

FIDO

Good dead are hard to find.

LIONSGATE PRESENTS AN ANAGRAM PICTURES PRODUCTION IN ASSOCIATION WITH TELEFILM CANADA A FILM BY ANDREW CURRIE "FIDO" CARRIE-ANNE MOSS BILLY CONNOLLY DYLAN BAKER INTRODUCING K'SUN RAY WITH HENRY CZERNY AND TIM BLAKE NELSON "MUSIC" JAN KISSER A.S.C. C.S.C. "EDITOR" ROB GRAY "PRODUCTION DESIGNER" ROGER MATTIUSSI "COSTUME DESIGNER" DON MACDONALD "MAKEUP" MARY E. McLEOD "CASTING" HEIDI LEVITT C.S.A. LYNNE CARROW C.S.A. "MUSIC" HEIDI LEVITT "EXECUTIVE PRODUCERS" PETER BLOCK JASON CONSTANTINE "CO-PRODUCERS" PATRICK CASSAVETTI SHELLEY GILLEN DANIEL IRON "PRODUCERS" TRENT CARLSON KEVIN EASTWOOD "PRODUCERS" BLAKE CORBET MARY ANNE WATERHOUSE "STORY" DENNIS HEATON "WRITTEN BY" ROBERT CHOMIAK & ANDREW CURRIE & DENNIS HEATON "DIRECTED BY" ANDREW CURRIE

R RESTRICTED UNDER 17 REQUIRES ACCOMPANYING PARENT OR ADULT GUARDIAN ZOMBIE RELATED VIOLENCE. www.lionsgate.com/fido CHUM LIONSGATE

Above: Film poster for Andrew Currie's *Fido* (2006).

Opposite: Dylan Baker, Billy Connolly, K'Sun Ray, and Carrie-Anne Moss in *Fido* (top); Fido (Connolly) and Helen (Moss) share a moment (bottom left); Timmy (Ray) and Fido (Connelly) encounter Cindy (Alexia Fast) (bottom right).

Romero's subversive narrative style seems to have inspired co-writer and director Andrew Currie's social satire *Fido* (2006). The Canadian film presents a utopian 1950s-era suburban society where zombies are exploited as domestic servants. When a housewife (Carrie-Anne Moss) brings one home, her introverted son Timmy (K'Sun Ray) makes a new best friend and names him Fido (Billy Connolly). When Fido's control collar malfunctions, he eats one of the neighbors, which causes a local zombie outbreak that undermines the idyllic community and jeopardizes his relationship with the boy and his mom.

Filmmakers Quentin Tarantino and Robert Rodriguez celebrated the exploitation films of the 1960s and '70s by attempting to re-create the B-movie experience for modern audiences with their double feature, *Grindhouse* (2007). "These kind of exploitation movies always seized on something that was happening during the day, even before Hollywood wanted to talk about them," Rodriguez said in an interview. "I thought, well, if I'm going to do a zombie movie then let's make it an infection that comes back from the Iraqi war, so that it's something that's current and something that people might fear." Rodriguez's tribute to the subgenre in his splatter-filled segment, *Planet Terror*, follows a group of survivors, including a go-go dancer (Rose McGowen) equipped with an M4 carbine leg prosthesis, who battle an onslaught of infected zombie-like townsfolk.

The millennial resurgence of the living dead also unearthed one of cinema's ultimate villains, the Nazis! A scattering of Nazi zombie movies began resurfacing toward the later part of the decade, beginning with the über-low-budget British production *Outpost* (2007), directed by Steve Barker. The film follows a group of mercenaries who are hired for a secret mission to a remote World War II–era military bunker where the Third Reich used to conduct occultist experiments. Before long, they're fighting for their lives against a barrage of undead Nazis. The film's success on DVD spawned the sequels *Outpost: Black Sun* (2012) and *Outpost: Rise of the Spetsnaz* (2013). In the Norwegian splatter-comedy *Dead Snow* (*Død Snø* [2009]), co-written and directed by Tommy Wirkola, a spring-break getaway in the mountains for a group of students is ruined by a platoon of rampaging Nazi SS zombies. "We just wanted to be the first in the whole of Scandinavia to make a zombie movie," said Wirkola. "So when we were about to sit down and write the actual script, we started thinking, 'What is more evil than a zombie—a Nazi zombie!'" The movie became a hit with audiences when it premiered at the Sundance Film Festival, where its sequel, *Dead Snow: Red vs. Dead* (*Død Snø 2* [2014]), also made its debut.

Above: Zombie-like townsfolk flourish in *Planet Terror* (2007); its movie poster features Cherry's (Rose McGowen) M4 carbine leg (below).

Opposite: Standartenführer Oberst Herzog (Ørjan Garnst) and his division of Nazi zombies (top); posters for *Dead Snow: Red vs. Dead* (*Død Snø 2*), and *Dead Snow* (*Død Snø* [2009]) (bottom).

Overleaf: *Dead Snow: Red vs. Dead* (*Død Snø 2* [2014]).

EN FILM AV TOMMY WIRKOLA

Official Selection 2014
sundance
film festival

HEIL FIVE!

DØD SNØ²

PÅ KINO 12. FEBRUAR

DEAD SNOW

a film by Tommy Wirkola

Above: Columbus (Jesse Eisenberg) must heed his own rules to survive *Zombieland* (2009).

Opposite: Theatrical poster featuring Woody Harrelson, Jesse Eisenberg, Emma Stone, and Abigail Breslin.

In 2009, Columbia Pictures heralded a new era for the subgenre with these few prophetic words from the opening voice-over of what became the biggest U.S.-grossing zombie picture to date, ". . . this is now the United States of Zombieland." As written by Rhett Reese and Paul Wernick, actor Jessie Eisenberg's dispiriting lines kick-start the R-rated action-comedy *Zombieland* (2009), playfully directed by Ruben Fleischer. Columbus (Eisenberg), a phobic nerd, tells us that he's managed to stay alive throughout the zombie apocalypse because of his endless list of rules. Rules like "Cardio," "Double Tap," "Check the Backseat," "Don't Be a Hero" read like a running list of zombie movie clichés, popping up as on-screen graphics at opportune moments for comedic effect. But his rules are put to the test when he sets out on a cross-country road trip with the zombie-killing redneck Tallahassee (Woody Harrelson) and two scam-artist sisters (Emma Stone and Abigail Breslin). While the rage-filled, fast-moving zombies they encounter and splatter to smithereens along the way take a page from *28 Days Later* (2002), their appetite for flesh is classic Romero. But before their film hit the big screen, scriptwriters Reese and Wernick had originally developed *Zombieland* for television. So naturally, after the film's historic mainstream success, Sony Pictures Television and Amazon Studios partnered to produce *Zombieland: The Series* (2013). But the unsuccessful twenty-nine-minute pilot didn't convince executives, who were initially enthusiastic in light of the high ratings and reception another zombie-themed series was receiving. That show, now a cross-platform franchise, has become one of the most popular shows on cable television—*The Walking Dead* (2010–).

WOODY HARRELSON
JESSE EISENBERG
EMMA STONE
ABIGAIL BRESLIN
ZOMBIELAND
NUT UP OR SHUT UP
COLUMBIA PICTURES PRESENTS IN ASSOCIATION WITH RELATIVITY MEDIA A PARIAH PRODUCTION "ZOMBIELAND" MUSIC BY DAVID SARDY
COSTUME DESIGNER MAGALI GUIDASCI EDITED BY PETER AMUNDSON ALAN BAUMGARTEN, A.C.E. PRODUCTION DESIGNER MAHER AHMAD DIRECTOR OF PHOTOGRAPHY MICHAEL BONVILLAIN
EXECUTIVE PRODUCERS EZRA SWERDLOW PAUL WERNICK RHETT REESE RYAN KAVANAUGH WRITTEN BY RHETT REESE & PAUL WERNICK PRODUCED BY GAVIN POLONE
DIRECTED BY RUBEN FLEISCHER
COLUMBIA PICTURES
R RESTRICTED
HORROR VIOLENCE/GORE AND LANGUAGE
IN THEATERS OCTOBER 9
Follow us @Zombieland on Twitter

Above: Columbus (Jesse Eisenberg) and Tallahassee (Woody Harrelson) form an un-likely pairing in *Zombieland*.

Opposite and Overleaf: Scenes from director Ruben Fleischer's *Zombieland.*

Above: Jenny Jones (Keisha Tillis) returns home in the premiere episode of *The Walking Dead* (2010).

Opposite: Poster for the first season of AMC's series.

Below: Special makeup effects artist Greg Nicotero touches up a walker on the set of *The Walking Dead*.

Zombies had now invaded television! The AMC original series *The Walking Dead*, based on writer Robert Kirkman and illustrator Tony Moore's ongoing post-apocalyptic comic books of the same name, premiered on October 31, 2010. Currently in its fifth season, the show has become one of the most-watched drama series in basic cable history and has received numerous primetime Emmy Awards and a Golden Globe nomination for best dramatic television series. "Apparently, now we're riding the crest of some sort of cultural wave," commented the show's creator, Frank Darabont. "It's the reminder that death is nipping at our heels." Darabont, an Academy Award–nominated writer-director known for *The Shawshank Redemption* (1994), wrote, directed, and executive produced the pilot, which closely resembles Romero's traditional zombie precepts, exploring the pitfalls of human nature. It follows sheriff deputy Rick Grimes (Andrew Lincoln), who awakens from a coma to discover a post-apocalyptic world overrun by flesh-eating zombies known as "walkers" or "biters." Grimes's search for his wife and son eventually leads him to a community of survivors, where he discovers they've been hiding with Shane Walsh (Jon Bernthal), his ex-partner and best friend. "I wish they would have called me," once joked Romero, who turned down an offer to direct an episode due to the close similarities to his own creation. Romero's *Day of the Dead* (1985) special makeup effects artist Greg Nicotero has directed several episodes, and his iconic zombie creations for the show have garnered multiple Emmy Awards. "I am so surprised that zombies have become as popular as they have become," remarked Darabont while promoting the first season of the show. "This was sub-sub-genre stuff. You had to be a real geek back, you know, back when the only magazine was *Famous Monsters*. You had to be a real geek to know even what a flesh-eating zombie was. Now, it's like, Grandma goes to the Barnes & Noble and buys the 'Zombie Survival Guide Joke Book' for her grandchildren, it's become so mainstream."

From the Director of **THE SHAWSHANK REDEMPTION** and the Producer of **THE TERMINATOR**

THE WALKING DEAD

A NEW ORIGINAL SERIES
SUNDAY OCT 31 10/9c **aMC**®

This Spread and Overleaf: Rick Grimes (Andrew Lincoln), Glenn (Steven Yeun), Andrea (Laurie Holden), Daryl (Norman Reedus), Shane (Jon Bernthal), Carol (Melissa McBride), Lori (Sarah Wayne Callies), and Carl (Chandler Riggs) in *The Walking Dead*.

Above: Poster for writer-director Alejandro Brujés's Cuban zombie epic.

Opposite: Lazaro (Jorge Molina) and Juan (Alexis Diaz de Villegas) confront a famished zombie populace on the streets of Havana in *Juan of the Dead* (*Juan de los Muertos* [2011]).

By 2010, zombies had fully crossed over into the mainstream all over the world, appearing in not only a wide range of big Hollywood studio movies, but also independent foreign films. Cuban filmmaker Alejandro Brujés wrote and directed *Juan of the Dead* (*Juan de los Muertos* [2011]), the first zombie movie shot on the Communist island. The bold social satire about a middle-aged slacker trying to eradicate the country's living dead infestation by starting a zombie-killing capitalist venture, pays tribute to the subgenre's classics and to Romero, specifically through its use of subversive wit. As Brujés once described, "Zombies are that part of Cuban society that is immobile and doesn't let things change—no matter in what direction."

Zombies could also be found in fun family fare, like Sony Pictures Animation's computer-generated mega-hit 'toon, *Hotel Transylvania* (2012), which was teeming with zombie bellhops. And the Academy Award–nominated, big-budget stop-motion horror-comedy *ParaNorman* (2012), about a young social outcast who must save his town when the dead begin to rise. Zombies were still scaring the teen demographic, too, with a major presence in Joss Whedon and Drew Goddard's monsterpalooza, *The Cabin in the Woods* (2012), a high-concept horror parody that initially appears to be a conventional genre film about a group of college students terrorized in a remote cabin. And there's director Jonathan Levine's "zom rom com," *Warm Bodies* (2013), a quirky post-apocalyptic love story told from the point of view of a zombie who begins coming back to life when he falls for a young female survivor. This zombie take on *Romeo and Juliet*, based on Isaac Marion's novel of the same name, went on to become one of the highest-grossing themed films.

IT'S ALL FUN AND GAMES UNTIL SOMEONE RAISES THE DEAD

8·17·12

PARANORMAN.COM

THE CABIN IN THE WOODS

Above: Norman hides while the zombie seeks (top); Dana (Kristen Connolly)

Opposite: Film poster for the *Romeo and Juliet*-inspired *Warm Bodies* (2013).

Above, right, and overleaf: R (Nicholas Hoult) and Julie (Teresa Palmer) in *Warm Bodies*.

MUSEUM OF NATURAL HISTORY
PRESENTS
4
3
2
Millions of years ago

OLUTION
The story of life

Above: Gerry Lane (Brad Pitt) protects his family from a global zombie invasion in *World War Z* (2013).

Opposite: Theatrical poster.

Just when the subgenre seemed to have finally reached widespread appeal, it achieved the pinnacle of Hollywood commercial validation with the PG-13 summer blockbuster release of Paramount Pictures' geo-political horror-thriller *World War Z* (2013), starring A-lister Brad Pitt. After a competitive bidding war no less, the studio purchased the movie rights to author Max Brooks's *New York Times* best-selling novel, *World War Z: An Oral History of the Zombie War* (2006), for Pitt's production company, Plan B Entertainment. The book reads like a credible collection of first-person accounts from around the world that describe the serious social and political fallout of the Zombie War. Brooks, a student of Romero's work, drew most of his zombie inspiration from the filmmaker's traditional canon, patterning the moaning, slow-moving, flesh-eaters as reanimated corpses infected by an incurable and contagious virus.

Crafting a screenplay that adapted the novel's collection of stories, while incorporating a central character, proved challenging. The script took years and underwent multiple drafts, with top Hollywood screenwriters J. Michael Straczynski, Matthew Michael Carnahan, Damon Lindelof, and Drew Goddard all contributing. Under the direction of Marc Forster, the film follows United Nations field agent Gerry Lane (Brad Pitt) and his family, as the zombie plague begins to infect the Eastern Seaboard of the United States and quickly spreads worldwide. To secure his family's safety, Lane reluctantly sets out for hotspots around the globe at the behest of the UN to hunt down patient zero and find a cure. The film's massive international scope, large-scale set pieces, and state-of-the-art digital effects set it apart from its lower-budget predecessors—and so do the flesh eaters themselves. Unlike in Brooks's novel, the film's thousands of zombies give chase and swarm en masse like giant ants, even taking down a chopper in one of the film's most iconic

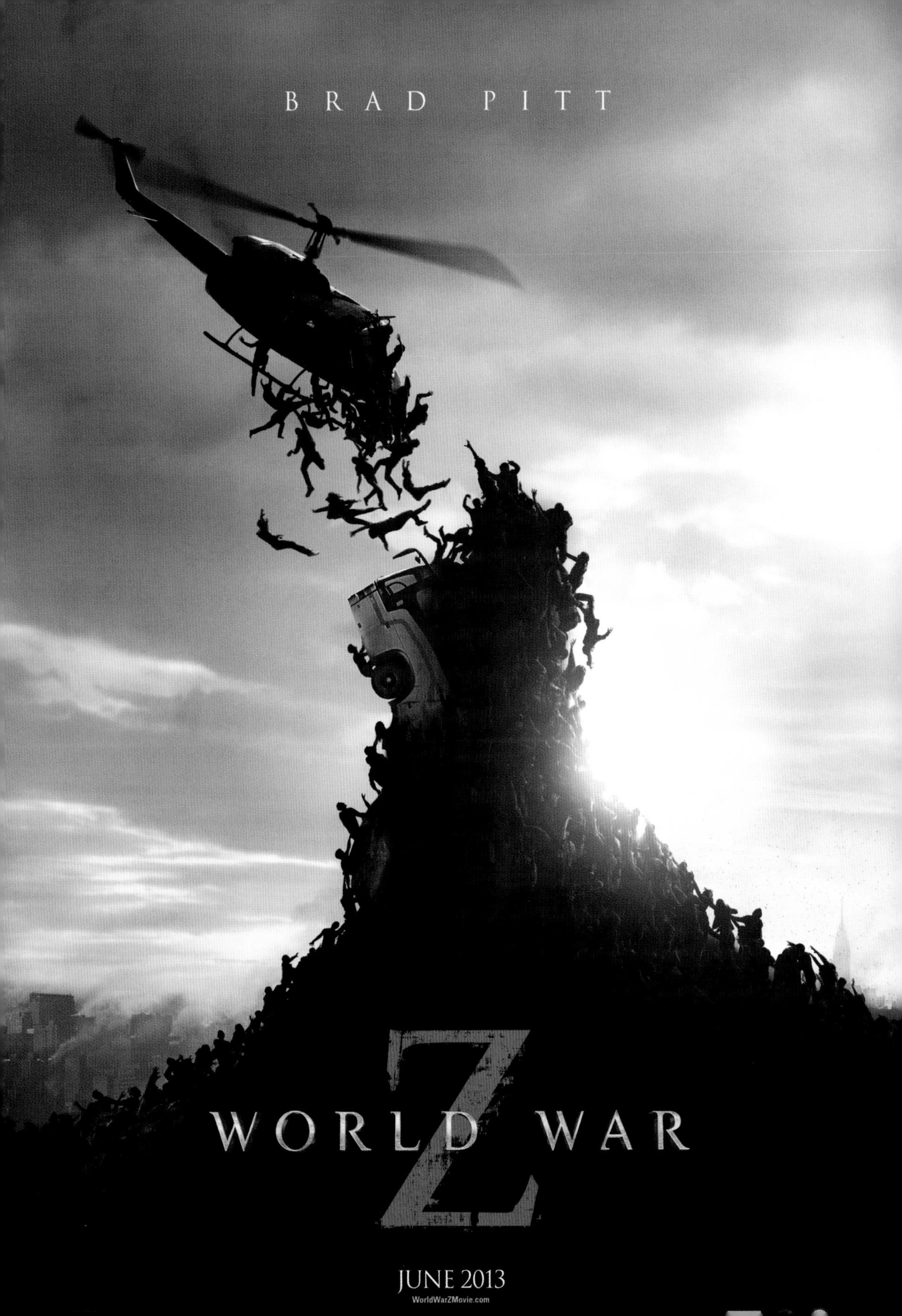
BRAD PITT
WORLD WAR Z
JUNE 2013
WorldWarZMovie.com

Jerins), Rachel (Abigail Hargrove), and Gerry (Bra[d] Pitt) stay together (top); U[N] Security General Thierry Umutoni (Fana Mokoena) takes charge (bottom) in *World War Z*.

Opposite: Gerry (Pitt) ta[kes] matters into his own hand[s] (top left); ex-CIA agent ([David] Morse) advises Gerry (Pit[t]) (top right) who barely ma[kes] out alive (bottom).

Overleaf: *World War Z'*[s] zombies swarm en masse [like] giant ants.

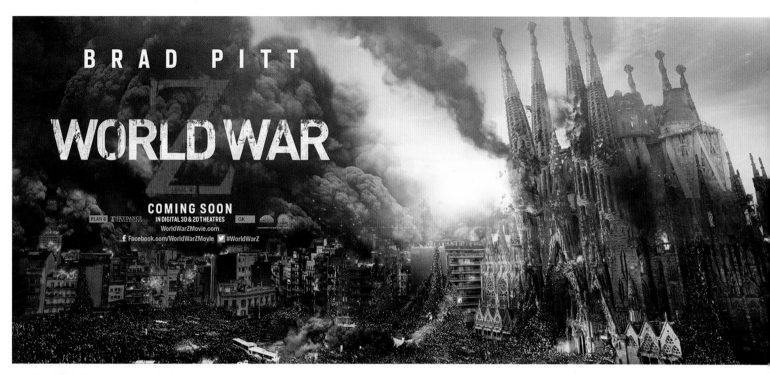

visuals. Besides the studio, the star, the spectacle, and the wide release, it was the lasting endurance of an eighty-year legacy that propelled *World War Z* and its zombie superstars to the heights of box-office success, earning over half a billion dollars and making it the largest-grossing zombie picture to date.

"THEY WON'T STAY DEAD!" proclaimed the theatrical poster for *Night of the Living Dead*. That prescient assertion has come to define zombies on film for over three-quarters of a century, where they will remain memorialized to entertain, thrill, and inspire future generations. Despite modifications to the canon, despite the diverse group of artists, styles, and genres, even despite the historical, cultural, and social shifts that occur over time, zombies will always be relevant and effective allegories, representing our inevitable fate—death. So when the lights dim and the movie begins, prepare to face your most primal fear. But rest assured that you will survive the carnage, perhaps even with a better understanding of the living, and for that we will all be forever beholden to those reanimated rotting corpses, to those ZOMBIES ON FILM.

Above: Banners from the international marketing campaign featured notable cities impacted by the zombie apocalypse.

Opposite: Israeli soldier Segen (Daniella Kertesz) and Gerry (Brad Pitt) barely escape the zombie onslaught.

Overleaf: Lobby card for *Night of the Living Dead* (1968).

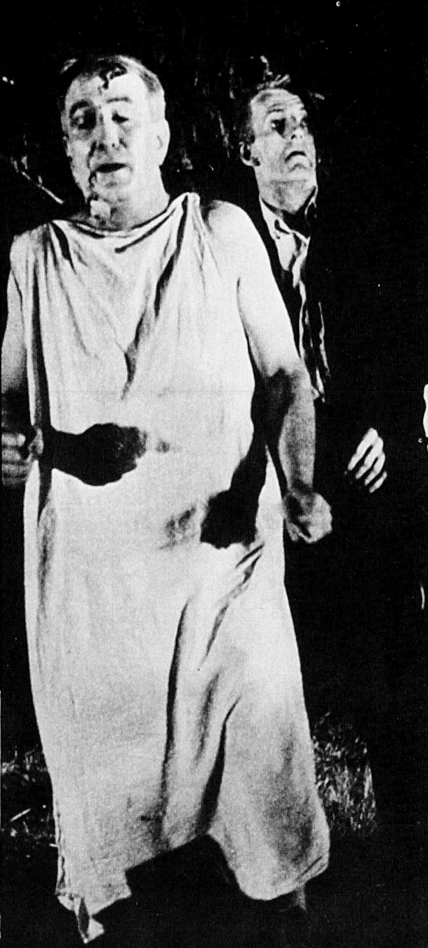

An IMAGE TEN Production

NIGHT OF THE LIVING DEAD

THEY WO

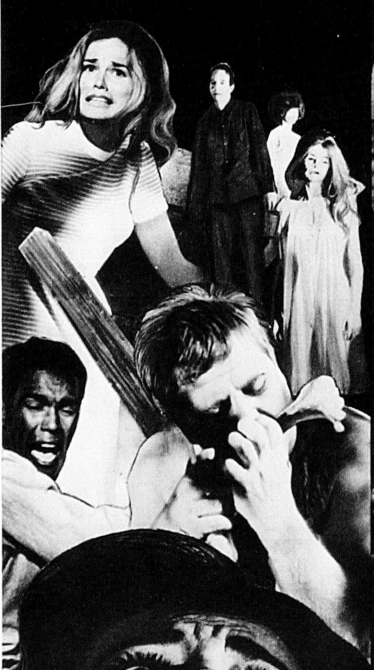

ON'T STAY DEAD!

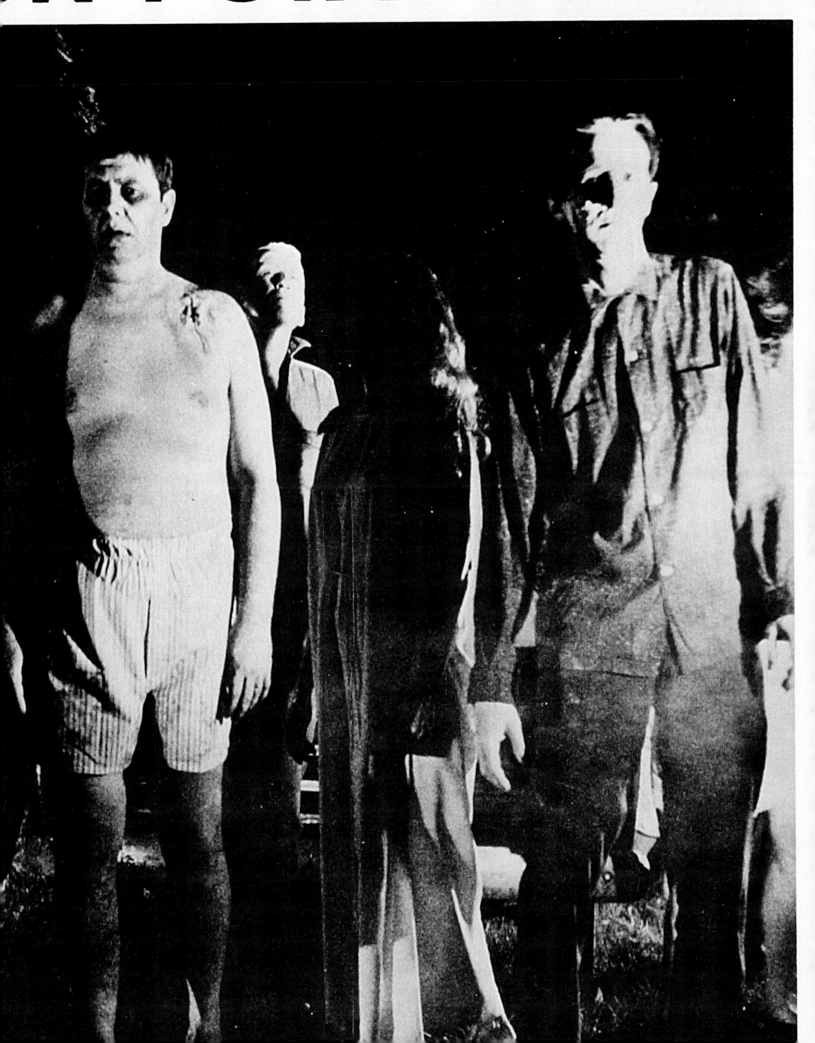

INDEX

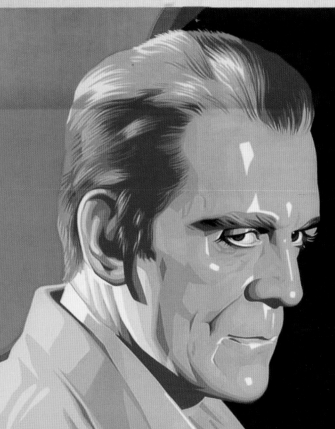

HE DIED
a man with
a hunger to
love . , . and
returned a
monster
with an in-
stinct to kill.

BORIS KARLOFF

in

"THE WALKING DEAD"

with

Ricardo CORTEZ

Edmund GWENN · Marguerite CHURCHILL
Warren HULL · Barton MacLANE
Henry O'NEILL · Joseph KING

Directed by MICHAEL CURTIZ

A
WARNER BROS.
PICTURE

5-9 3/36
MADE IN U.S.A.

CAN YOU SURVIVE THIS
ORGY OF THE LIVING DEAD?

A TRIPLE AVALANCHE OF
GRISLY HORROR!

ALL IN COLOR!

PG
PARENTAL GUIDANCE
May not be suitable
for pre-teenagers

WARNING!

1st Hit
Revenge of the Living Dead

2nd Hit Mario Bava's
Curse of the Living Dead

3rd Hit
Fangs of the Living Dead
with Anita Ekberg

A EUROPIX-INTERNATIONAL LTD. RELEASE

This is John Austin Frazier. It has been reported that he now resides at a Mental Hospital, the result of attending a showing of our triple horror program, ORGY OF THE LIVING DEAD! Because of this tragic event, we, the producers, have secured an insurance policy insuring the sanity of each and every patron. If you lose your mind as a result of viewing this explosion of terror, you will receive free psychiatric care or be placed, at our expense, in an asylum for the rest of your life! We urge you to take advantage of this protection! The insurance is free - anyone entering the theatre without it does so at his own risk. Remember **WE WARNED YOU!!!**

72/410

ORGY OF THE **LIVING DEAD**